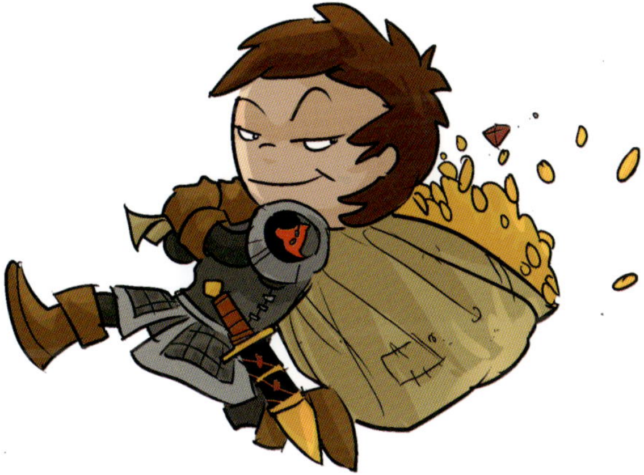

To all those who love the grand adventure, the long nights, and the roll of the dice ... may your rolls be critical.

Copyright © 2017 All Rights Reserved, Travis Hanson & Bean Leaf Press. Unauthorized reproduction except for the purpose of review is prohibited by law. Title logo, Bean Leaf Press Logo and all Life of the Party characters and art are copyright © 2017 by Travis Hanson.

For contact information, subscription or letters to the artist, please send all inquiries to
Bean Leaf Press
P.O. Box 6495
Moreno Valley CA 92554

Hardcover ISB978-1-64007-509-2
Printed in China
Forward by Tony Parker

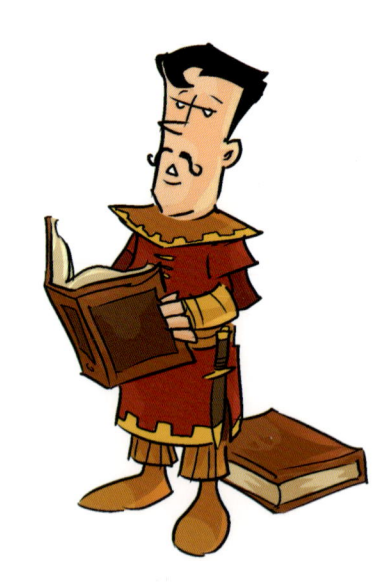

Life of the Party
the Realities of an RPG'er

created by Travis Hanson
Forward by Tony Parker

18/00

That's how long I've been playing tabletop role playing games. The old school gamers recognize that set of numbers. It means 18/00 strength, which is the maximum that a nonmagical human can get. I got it off a straight roll for my very first rolled RPG character, and that is more years ago than I care to admit to. I've been playing tabletop RPG's ever since, and loving every minute of it.

I've been playing with the same group of gamers for many years now. During a session, I looked over and saw a picture of a dwarf in armor floating in a green cube. I recognized that image right away. I asked him where he got it, and he responded he found it online on a friend's page. He loved it, and had to make it his phone wallpaper. I smiled, admitting that I knew the artist. My friend loved that art, and asked who did it. I told him. Travis Hanson.

I've known Travis for quite some time as well. We met back when the local Phoenix convention was a small, 2,000 person show. I don't remember the first conversation, or the second, but I remember a lot of the ones since then. His heart is greater than a colossal dragon, his smile brighter than enchanted armor, and his friendship more valuable than magical rings (and not cursed). He's loved the fantasy genre for years, as is shown by his Eisner-nominated Bean webcomic. His love of humanity is shown every time he interacts with any person.

He loves drawing, and posting fantasy art. We've all loved seeing his new take on classic genres, or catching that perfect moment that anyone who has played RPGs recognizes immediately. This book that you are currently reading contains many of these drawings. The drawings hold strong themselves, being delightfully lighthearted and recognizing the delightful absurdity of the dangers of the fantasy RPG. Should you come across a drawing in which you don't get the joke, just keep playing RPGs. You will, and you will appreciate the drawing all the more.

For those of you just starting out with playing RPGs, there are a few solid pieces of

ADVICE FOR YOU TO FOLLOW. IN A DUNGEON, LEFT IS ALWAYS RIGHT. CARRY AT LEAST ONE WOODEN WEAPON AND SHIELD. PROTECT THE HEALER. ALWAYS USE YOUR OFF HAND TO GRAB THINGS. THE SYSTEM DOESN'T MATTER IF YOU HAVE A GOOD GROUP. **NEVER** SPLIT THE GROUP, ESPECIALLY IF YOU HAVE SOMEONE LIKE TRAVIS WITH YOU.

THANKS!
TONY PARKER

ARTIST IN 150+ RPG BOOKS, 132 CCG CARDS, EISNER NOMINATED COMIC BOOK ARTIST, AND THAT GUY WHO NAMES ALL OF HIS CHARACTERS WITH NAMES THAT MAKE EVERYONE ELSE CRINGE.

PS-THAT CHARACTER, BOB THE EXECUTIONER, HAD A 6 INTELLIGENCE, AND A SWORD WITH 16 INTELLIGENCE. TRAIN WRECKS ARE FUN.

Life of the Party: Realities of an RPG'er

by Travis Hanson

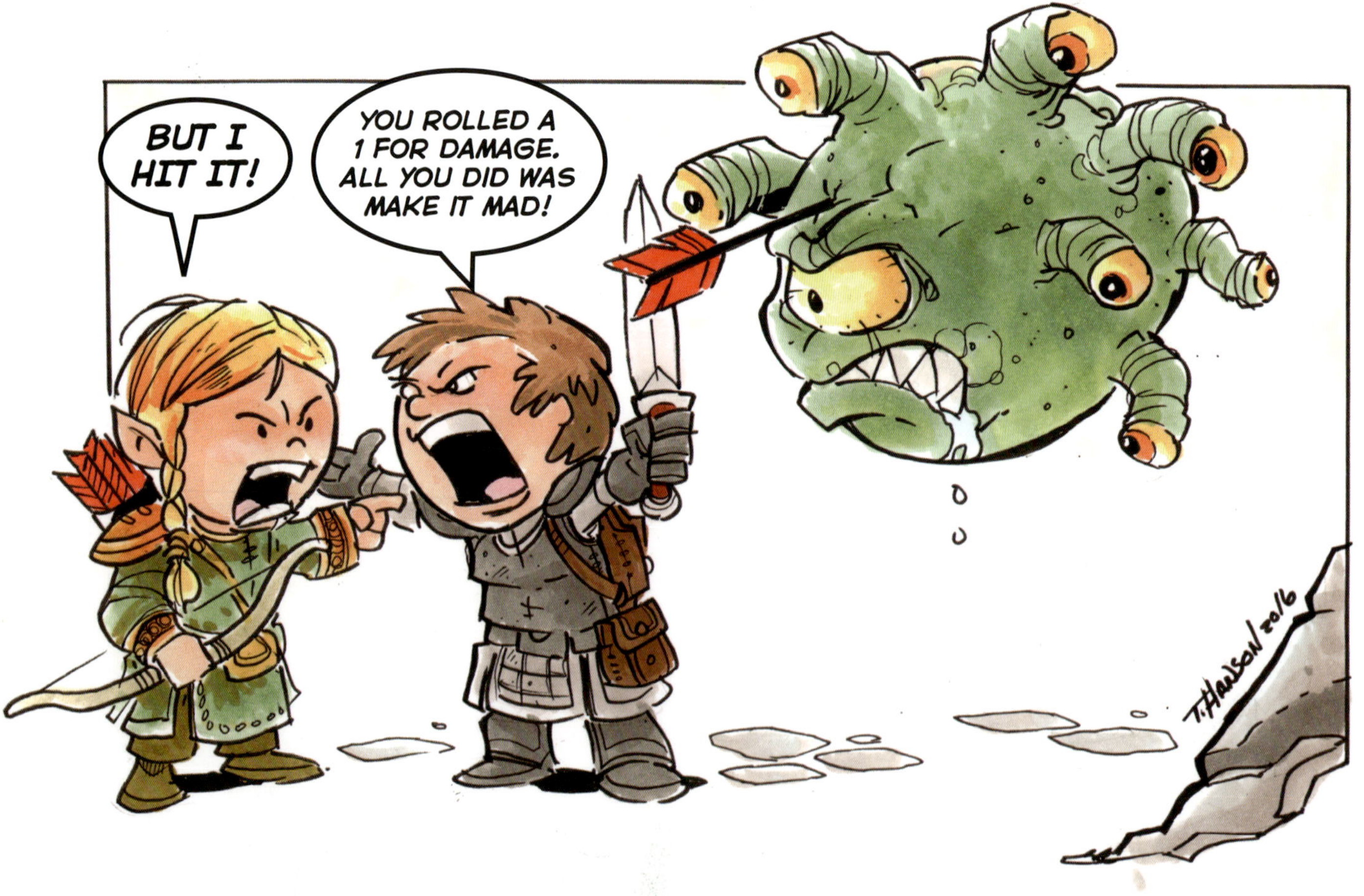

Life of the Party: Realities of an RPG'er

by Travis Hanson

Life of the Party: Realities of an RPG'er

by Travis Hanson

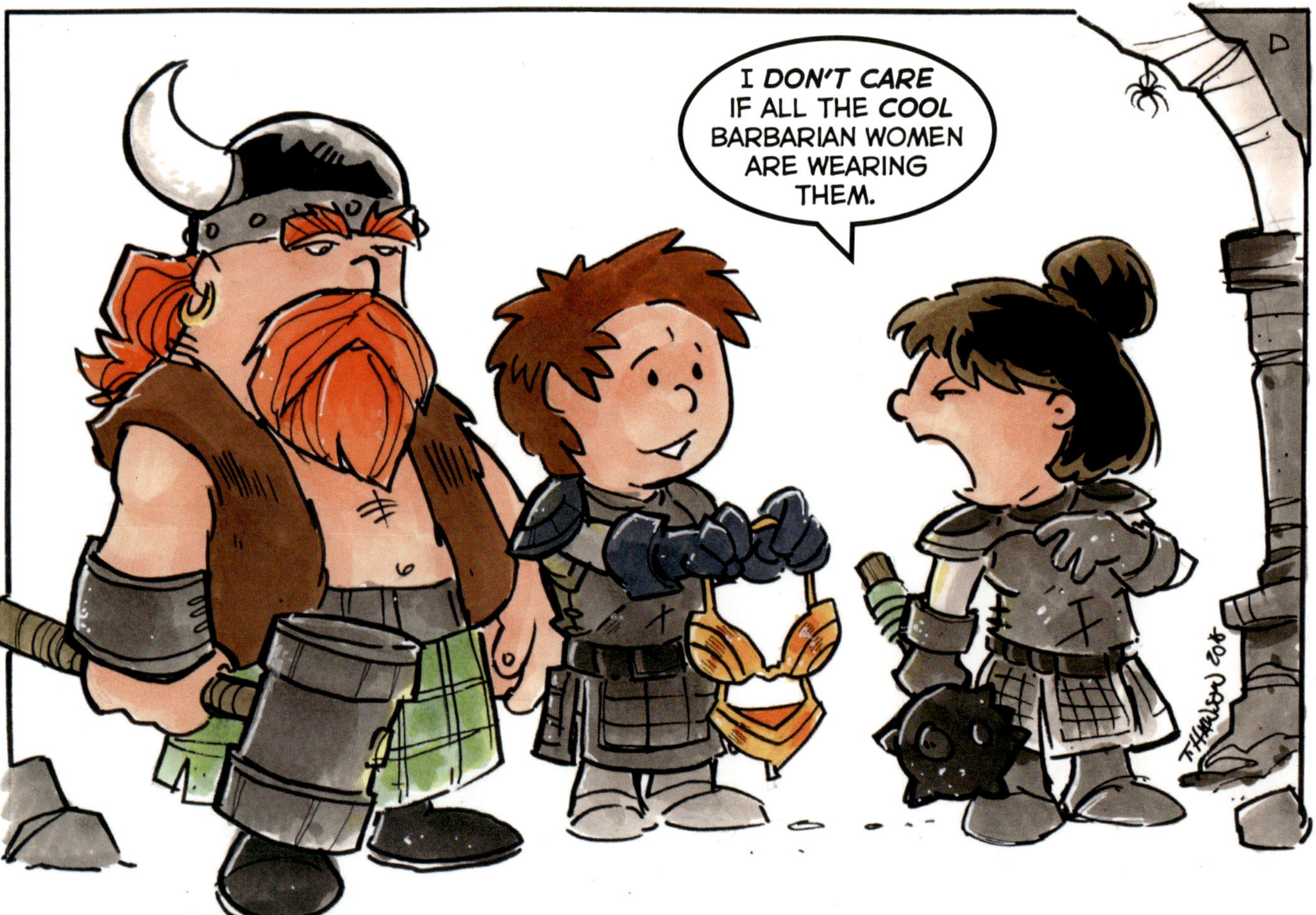

Life of the Party: Realities of an RPG'er by Travis Hanson

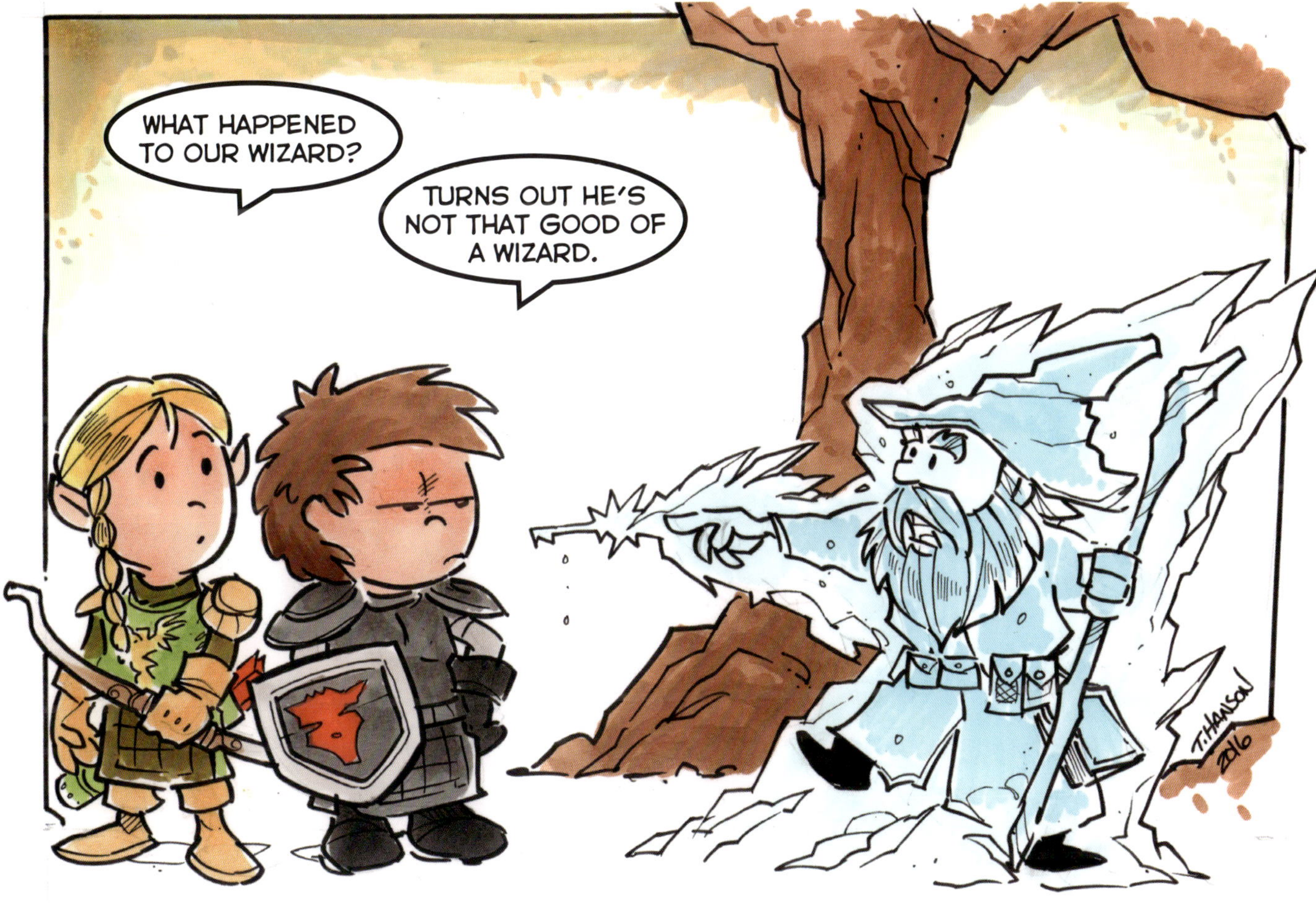

Life of the Party: Realities of an RPG'er

by Travis Hanson

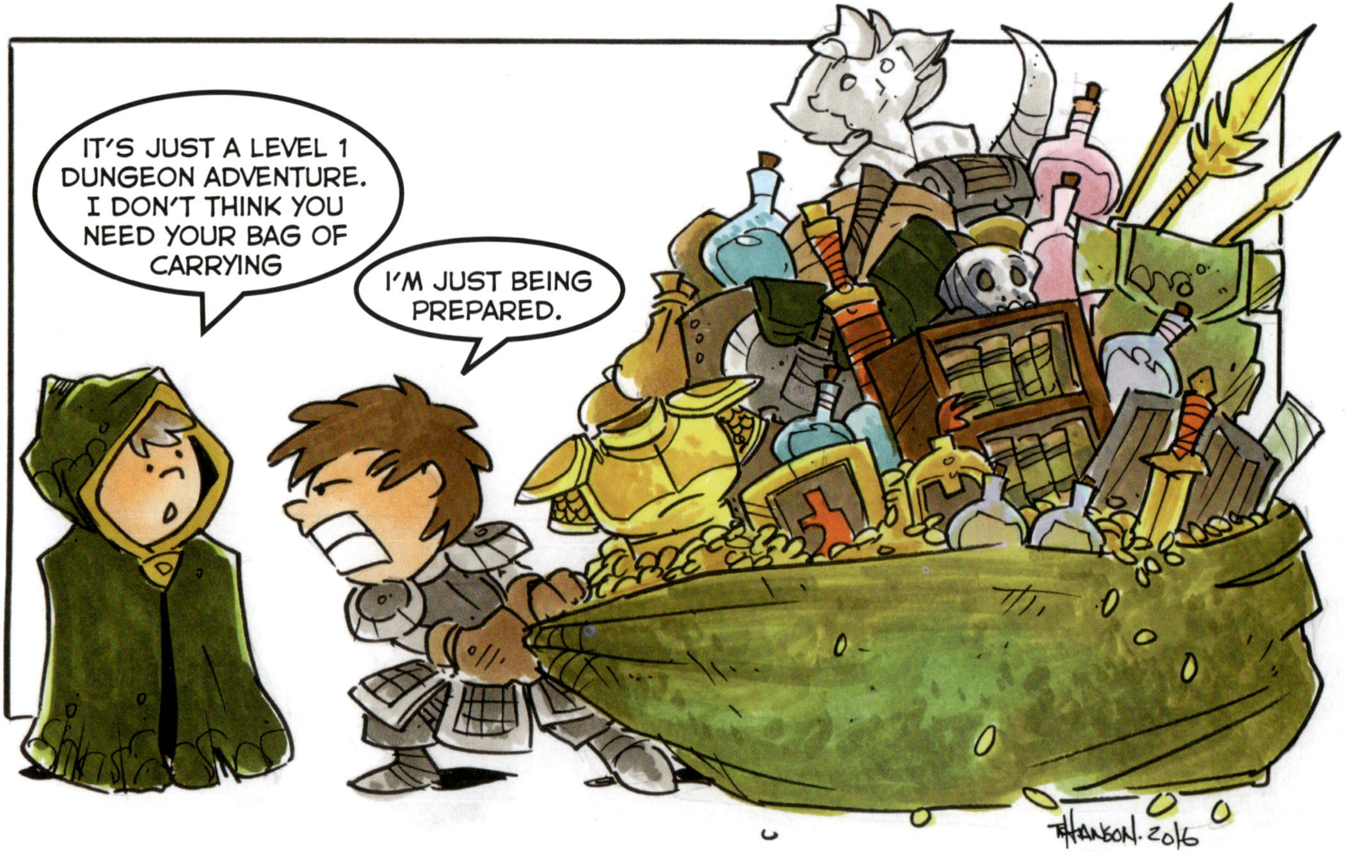

Life of the Party: Realities of an RPG'er

by Travis Hanson

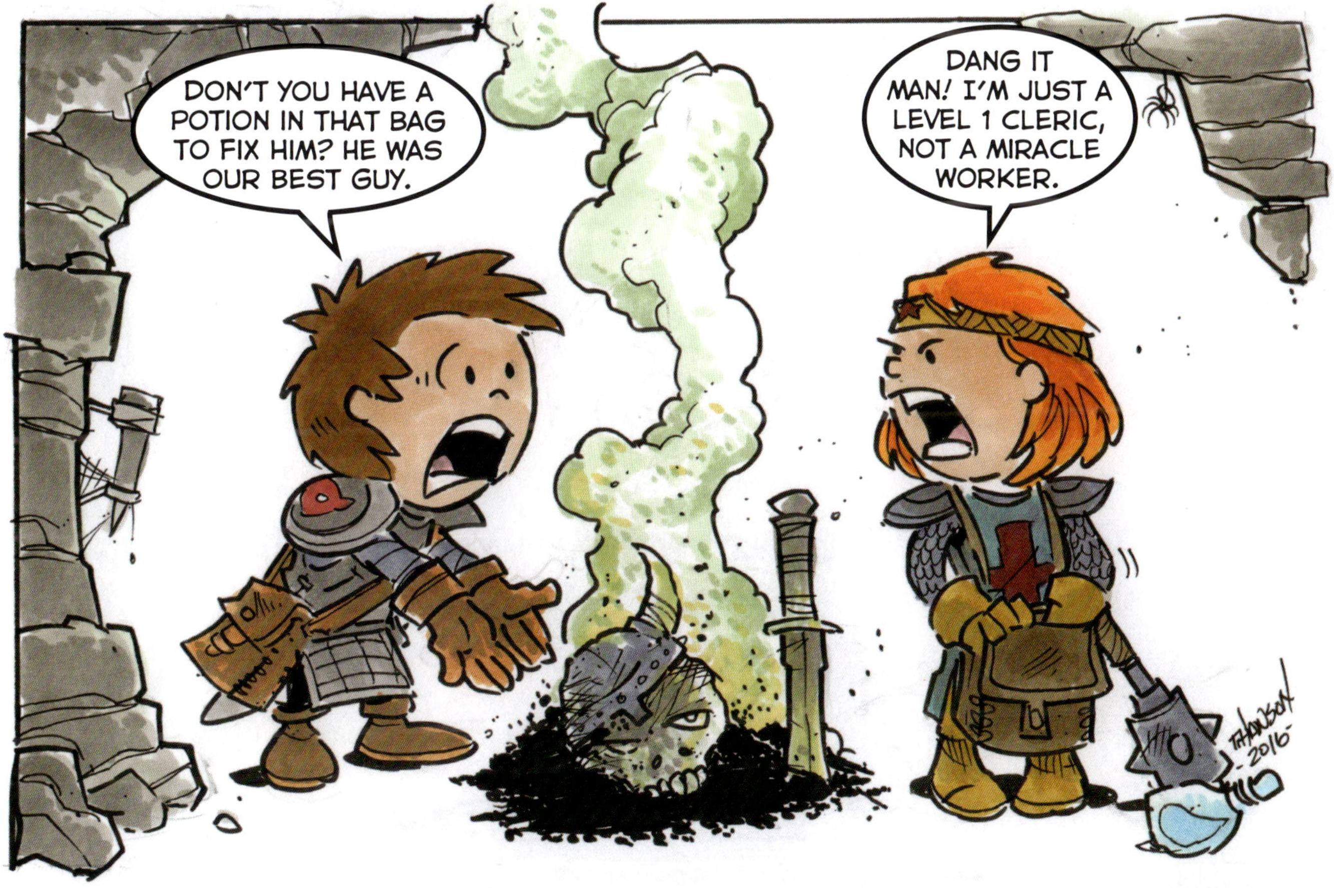

Life of the Party: Realities of an RPG'er
by Travis Hanson

"OK, BEFORE I GO OUT AND CHECK ON THAT NOISE, I'M GONNA HIDE THIS +5 VORPAL SWORD OF SLAYING AND THIS BAG OF GOLD IN THIS TRASH PILE HERE. YOU GUYS JUST HANG OUT 'TIL I GET BACK."

Life of the Party: Realities of an RPG'er — by Travis Hanson

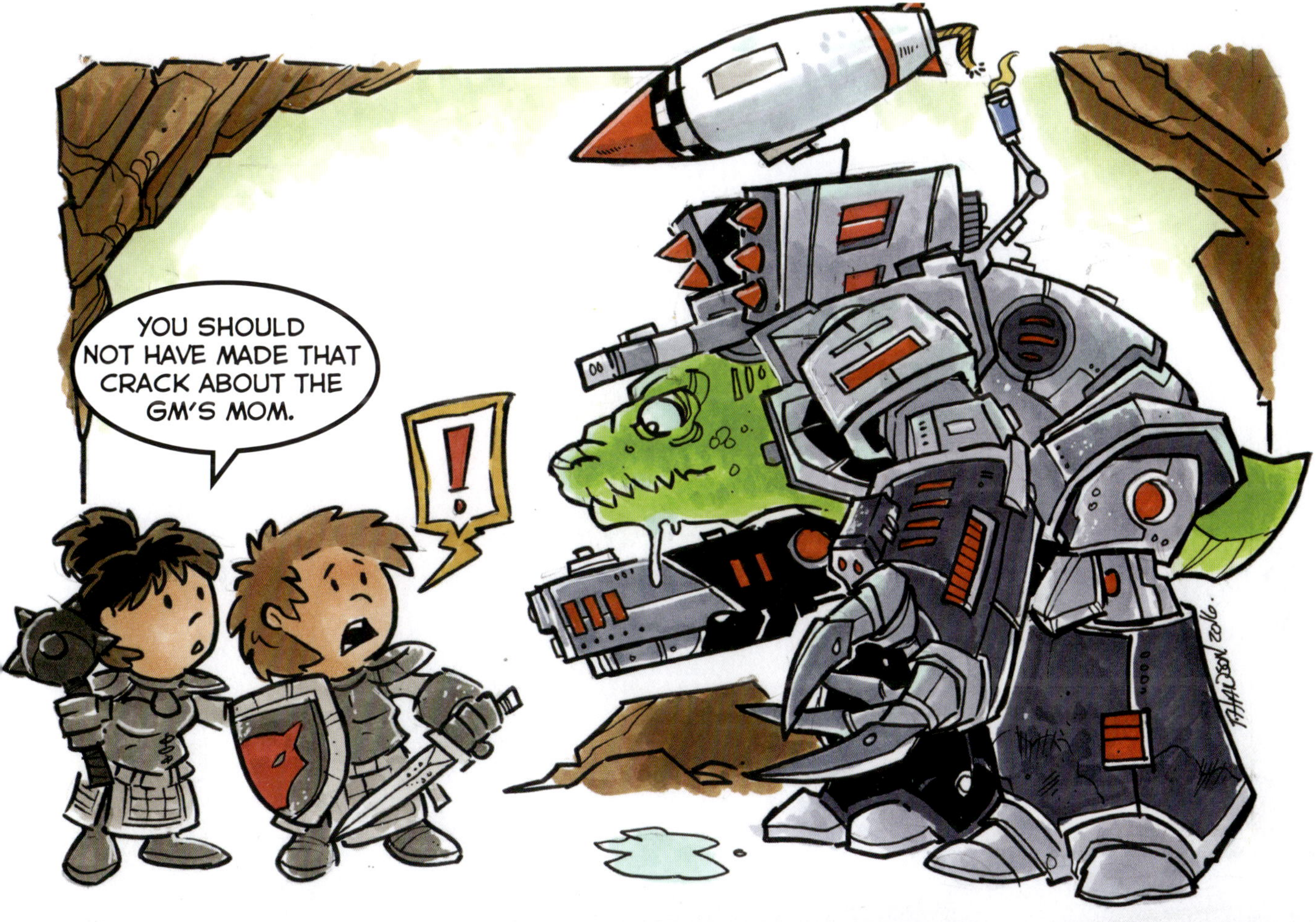

Life of the Party: Realities of an RPG'er

by Travis Hanson

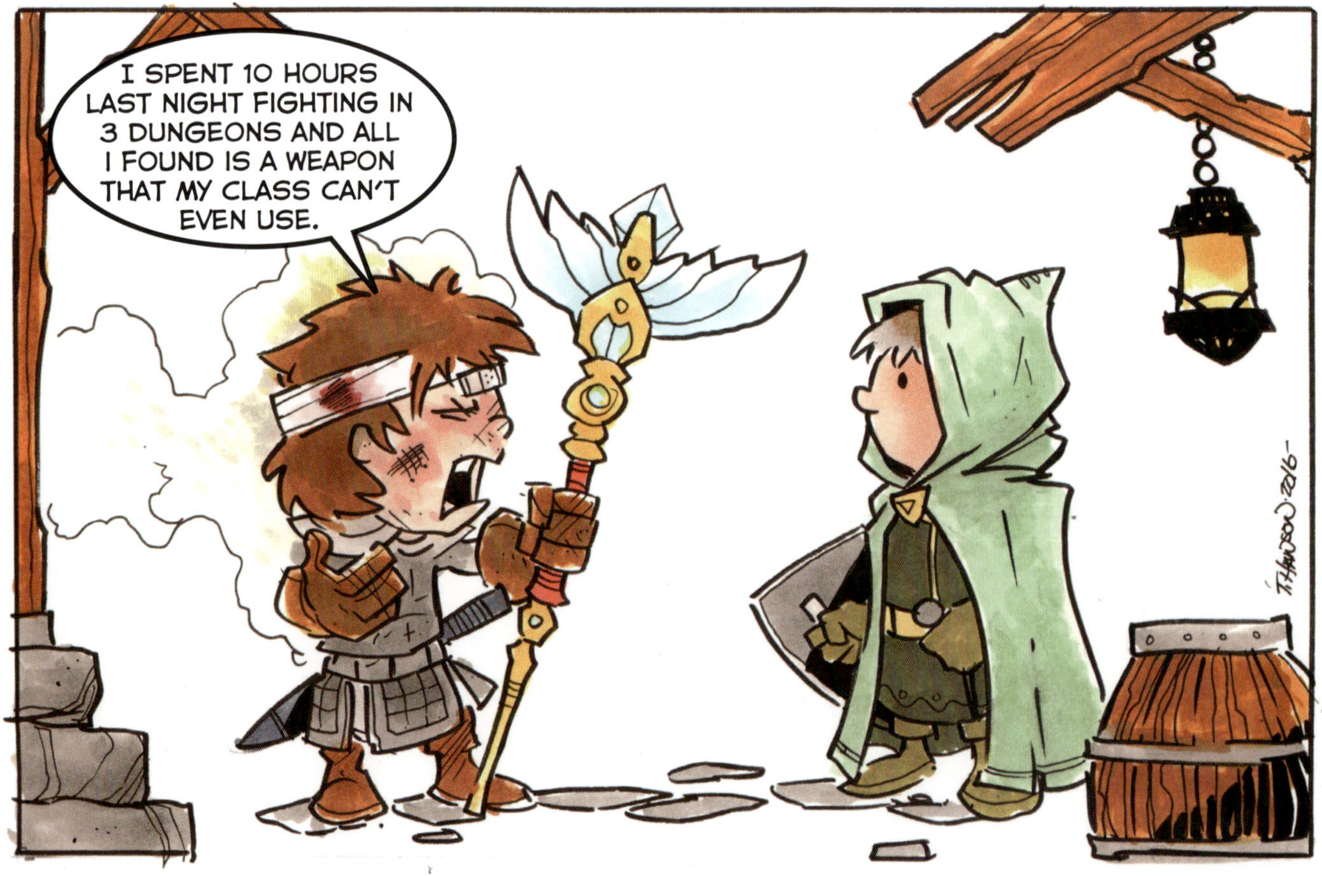

Life of the Party: Realities of an RPG'er

by Travis Hanson

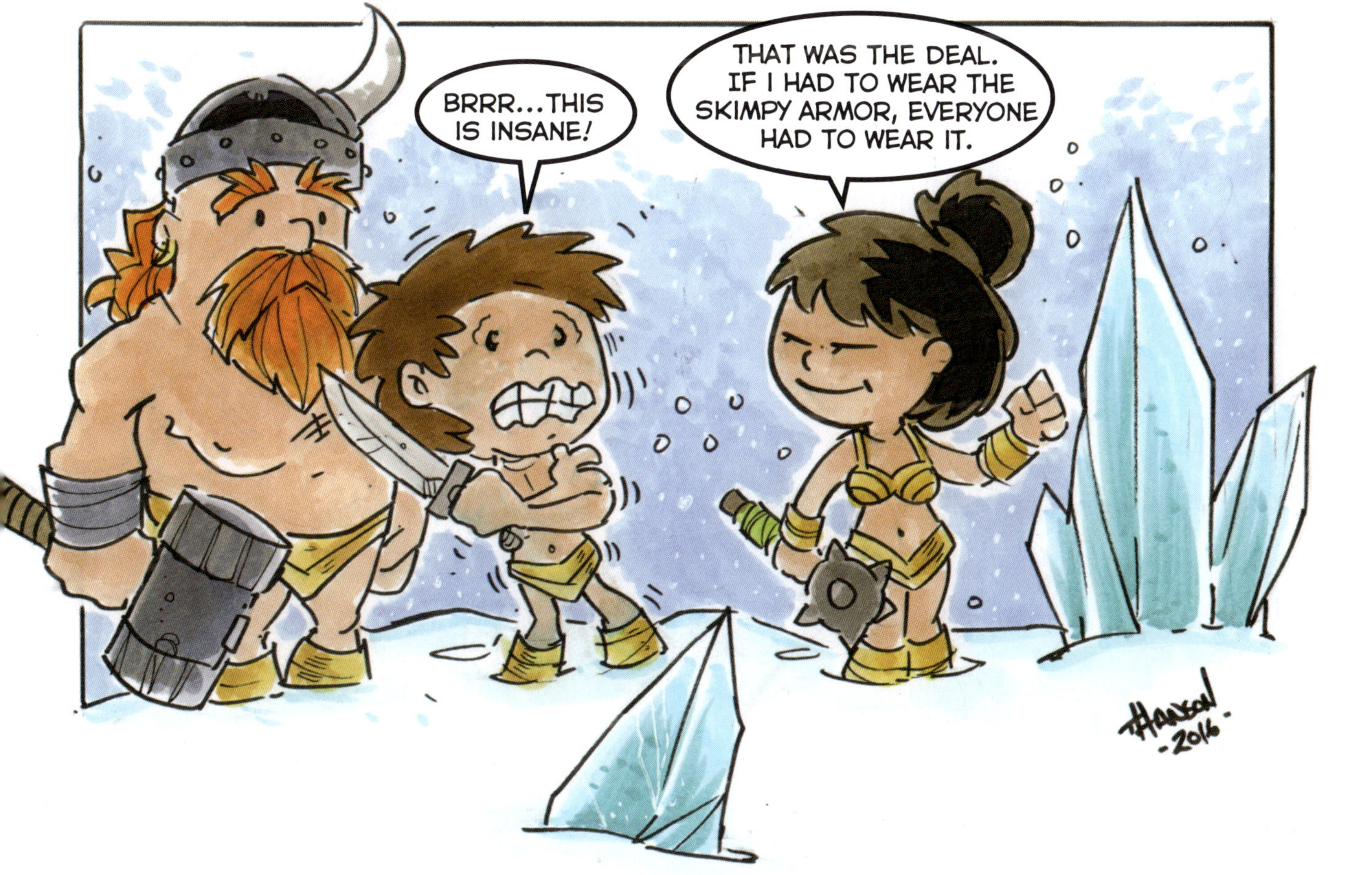

Life of the Party: Realities of an RPG'er

by Travis Hanson

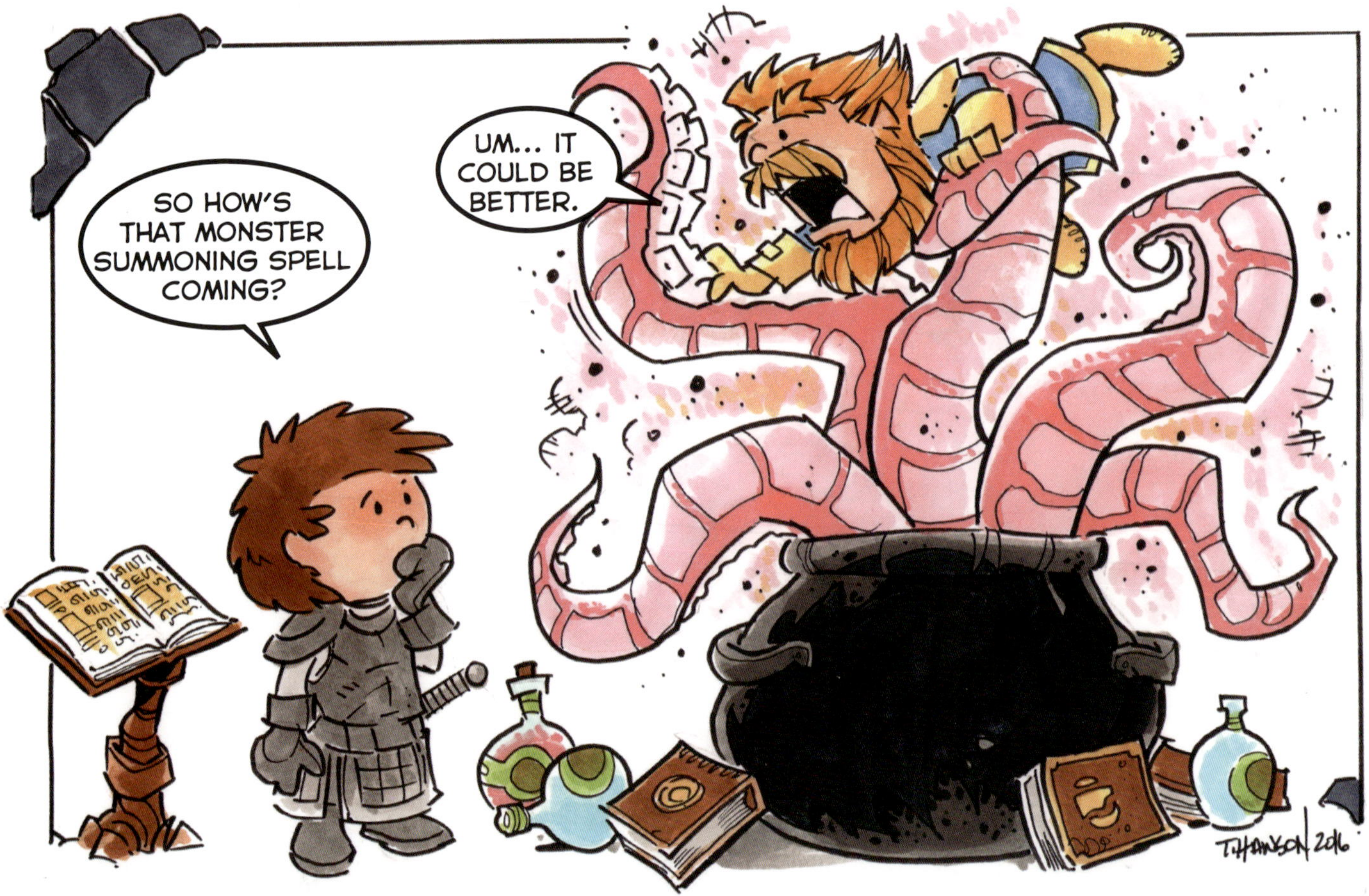

Life of the Party: Realities of an RPG'er

by Travis Hanson

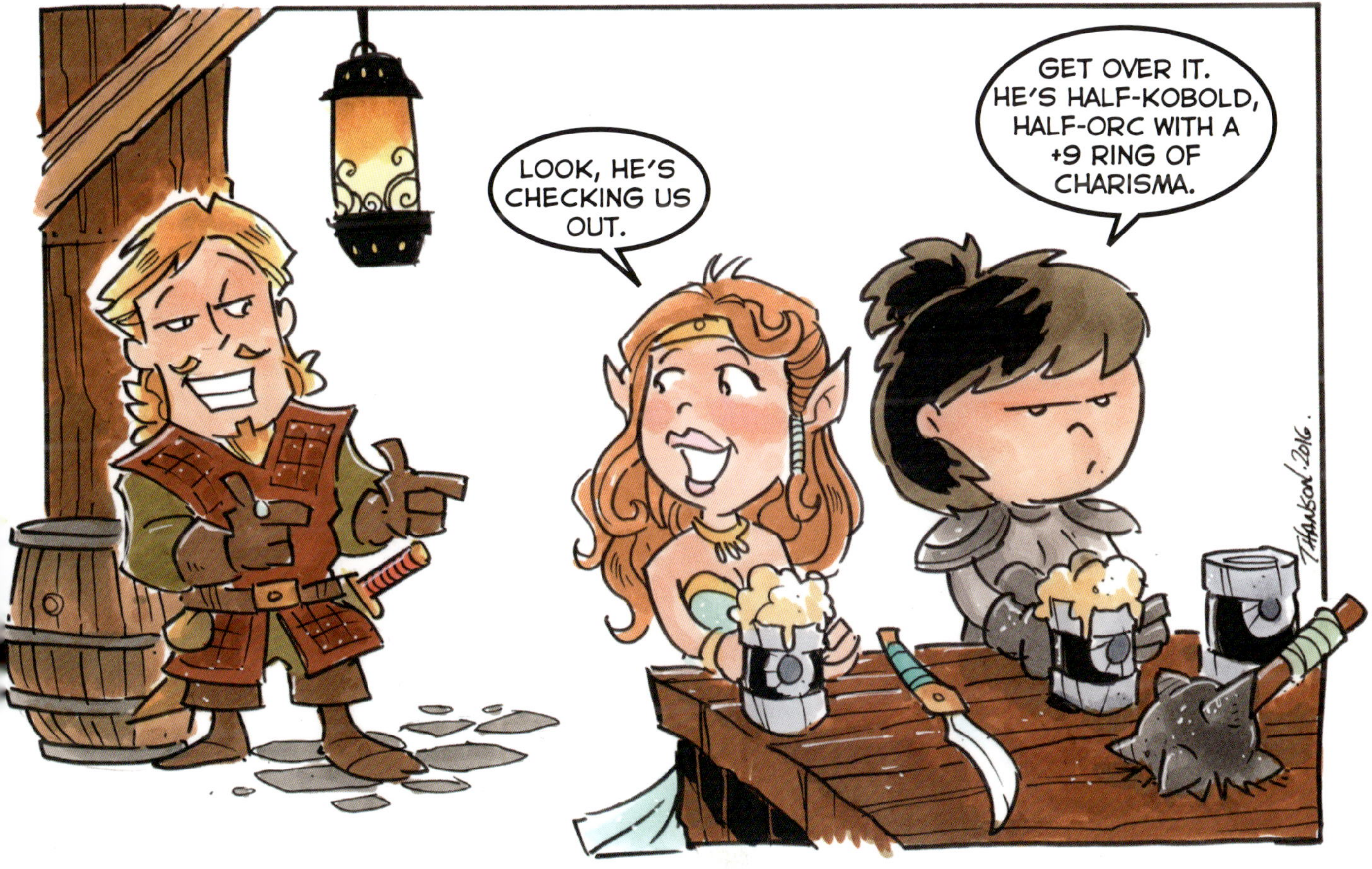

Life of the Party: Realities of an RPG'er
by Travis Hanson

OH GREAT AND POWERFUL GM. MAY YOU HAVE PITY ON MY SOUL THAT I MIGHT BE ABLE TO SURVIVE THIS CAMPAIGN AND FILL MY POCKETS WITH LOTS OF GOLD AND MAGIC ITEMS. SO, I OFFER THIS BAG OF CHEETOS, A SIX PACK OF SODA, AND SOME SKITTLES TO PLEASE THEE AND ENSURE MY CHANCES FOR SURVIVAL.

Life of the Party: Realities of an RPG'er

by Travis Hanson

I JUST FOUND 265 GOLD PIECES.
I PERSONALLY DON'T WANT TO KNOW WHERE HE WAS HIDING IT.
T.HANSON·2016

Life of the Party: Realities of an RPG'er
by Travis Hanson

Knight: ARE YOU OK?

Warrior: YUP, NUTHIN A FEW POTIONS AND A BOTTLE OF MEAD WON'T CURE.

Life of the Party: Realities of an RPG'er
by Travis Hanson

by Travis Hanson

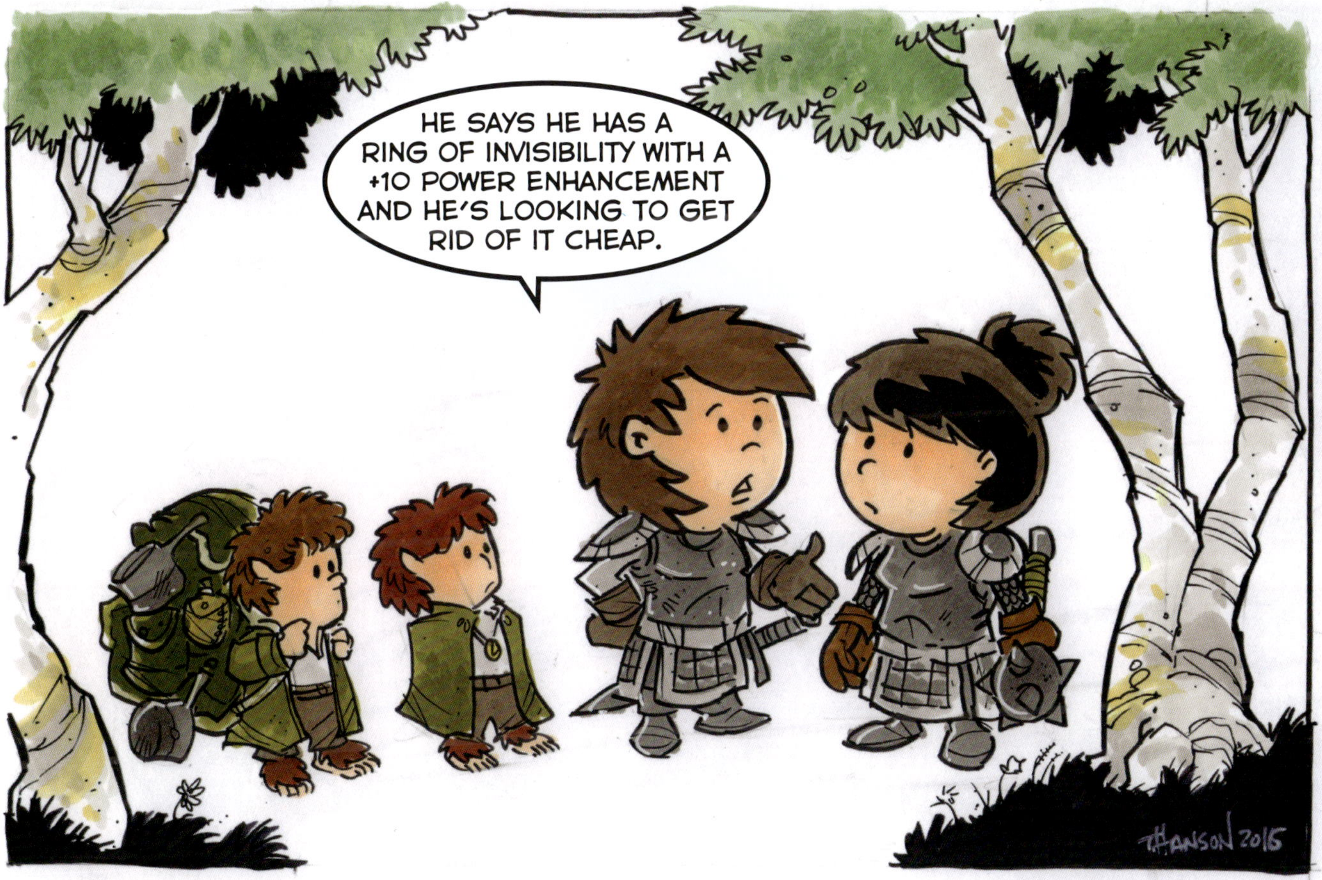

Life of the Party: Realities of an RPG'er

by Travis Hanson

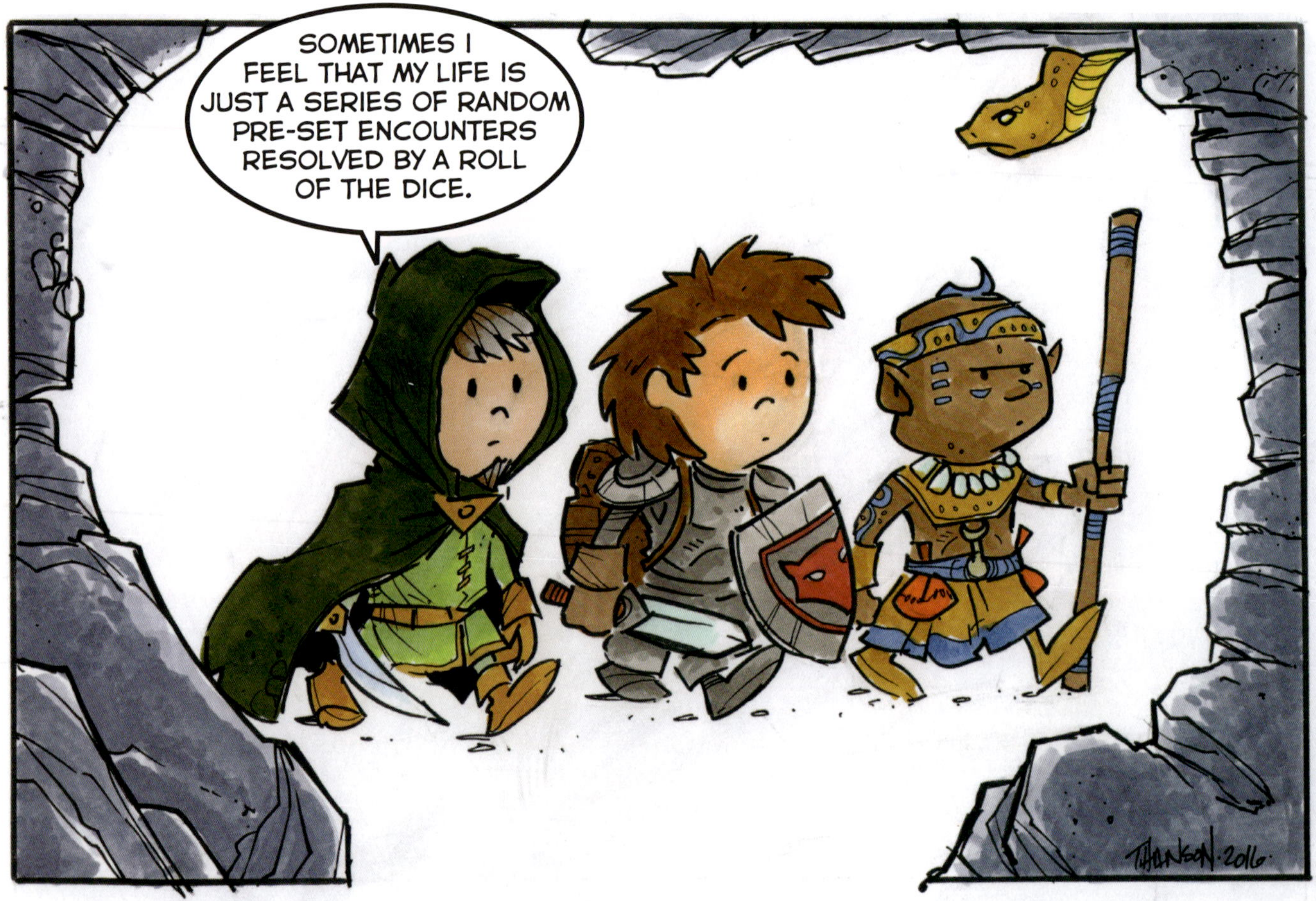

Life of the Party: Realities of an RPG'er

by Travis Hanson

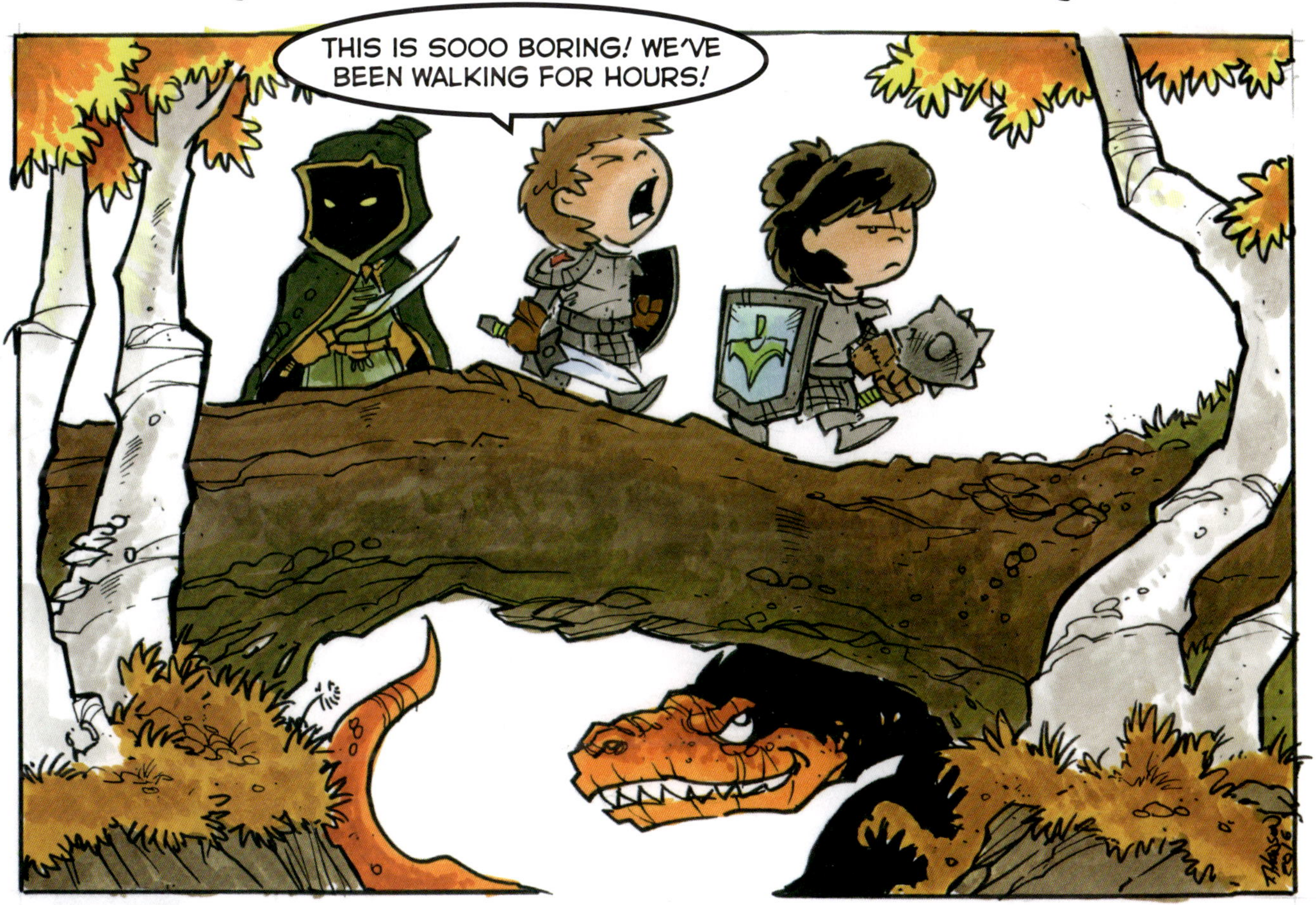

Life of the Party: Realities of an RPG'er

by Travis Hanson

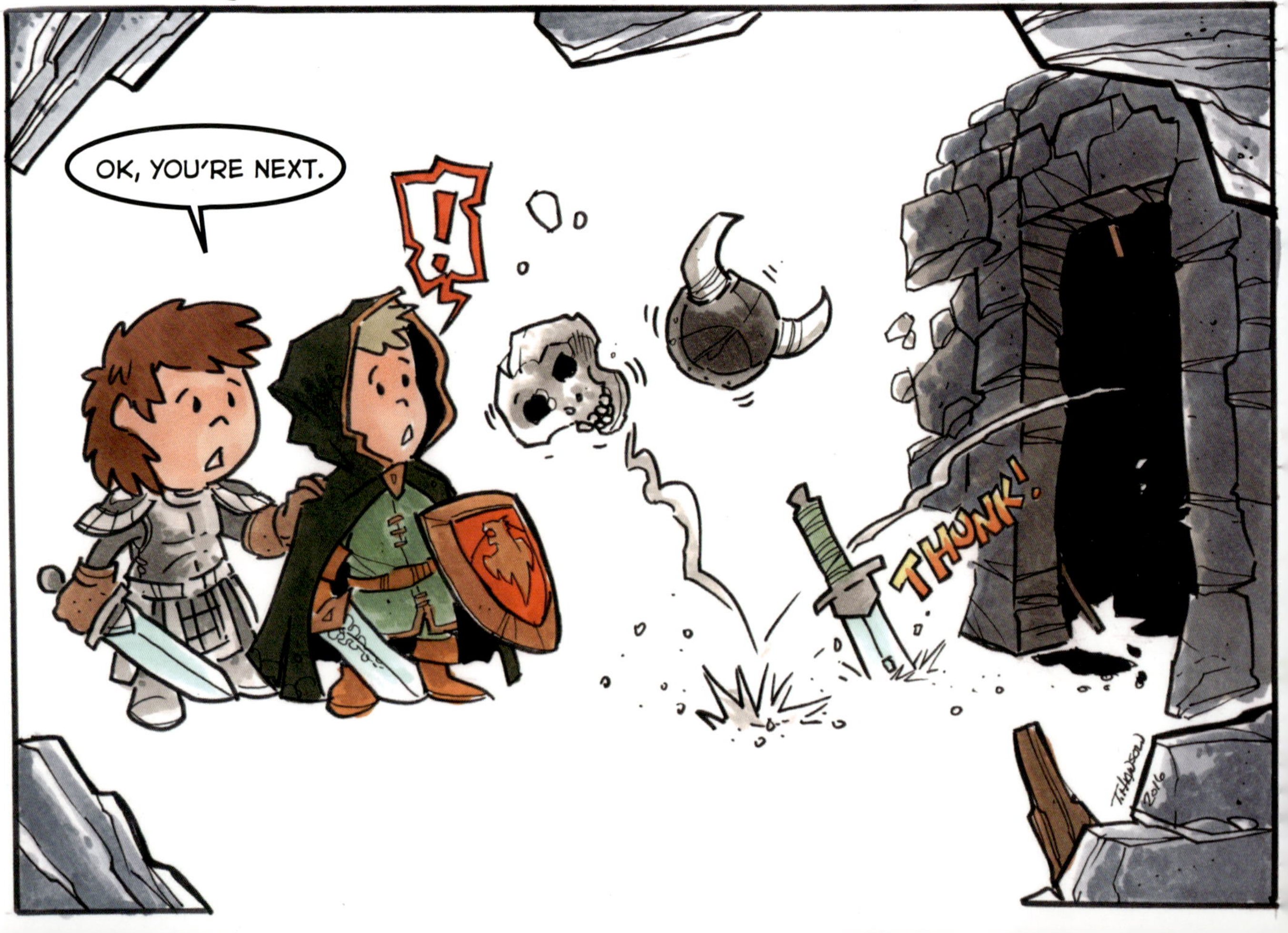

Life of the Party: Realities of an RPG'er

by Travis Hanson

Life of the Party: Realities of an RPG'er — by Travis Hanson

Life of the Party: Realities of an RPG'er

by Travis Hanson

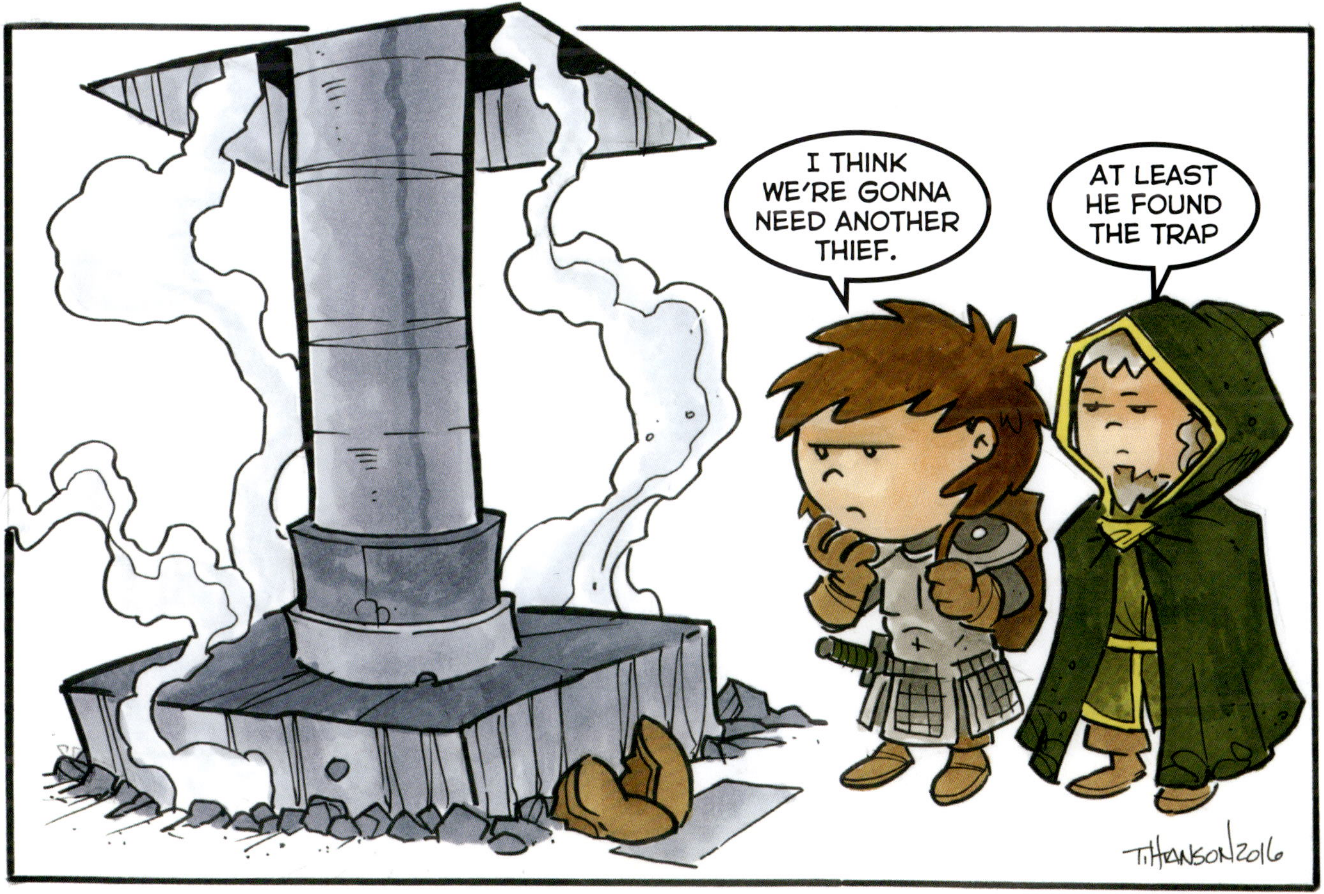

Life of the Party: Realities of an RPG'er — by Travis Hanson

Life of the Party: Realities of an RPG'er

by Travis Hanson

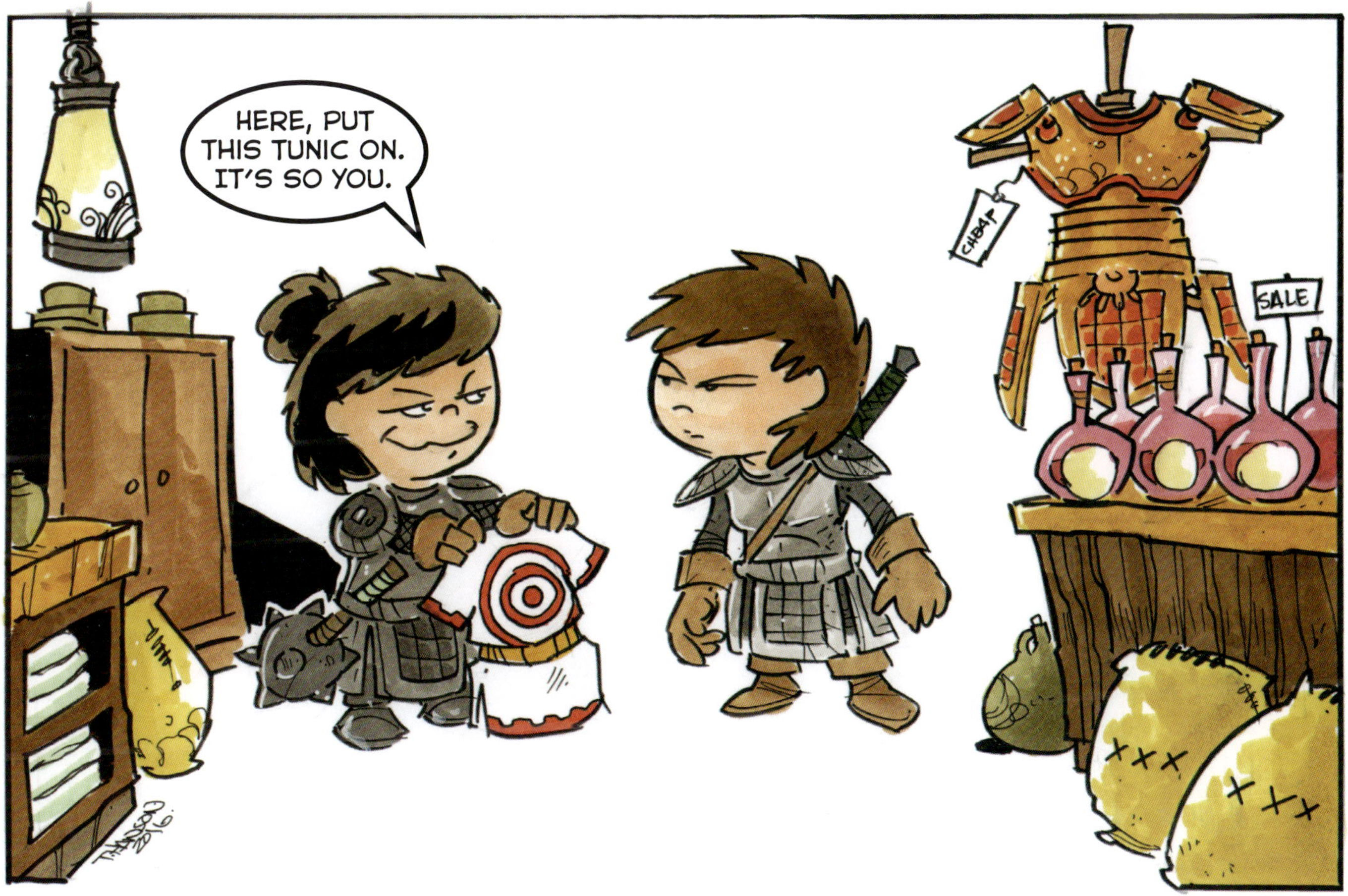

Life of the Party: Realities of an RPG'er

by Travis Hanson

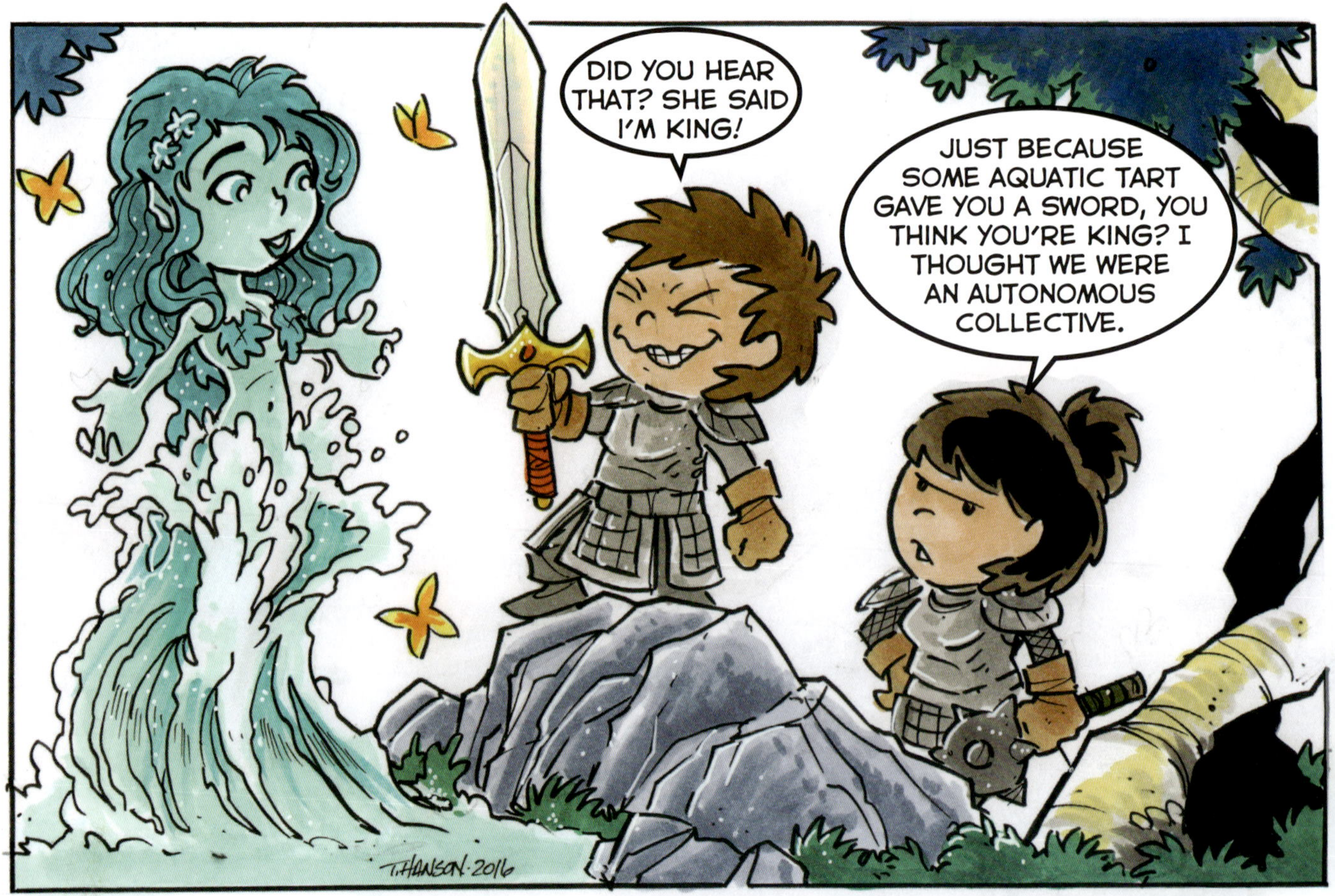

Life of the Party: Realities of an RPG'er — by Travis Hanson

Life of the Party: Realities of an RPG'er

by Travis Hanson

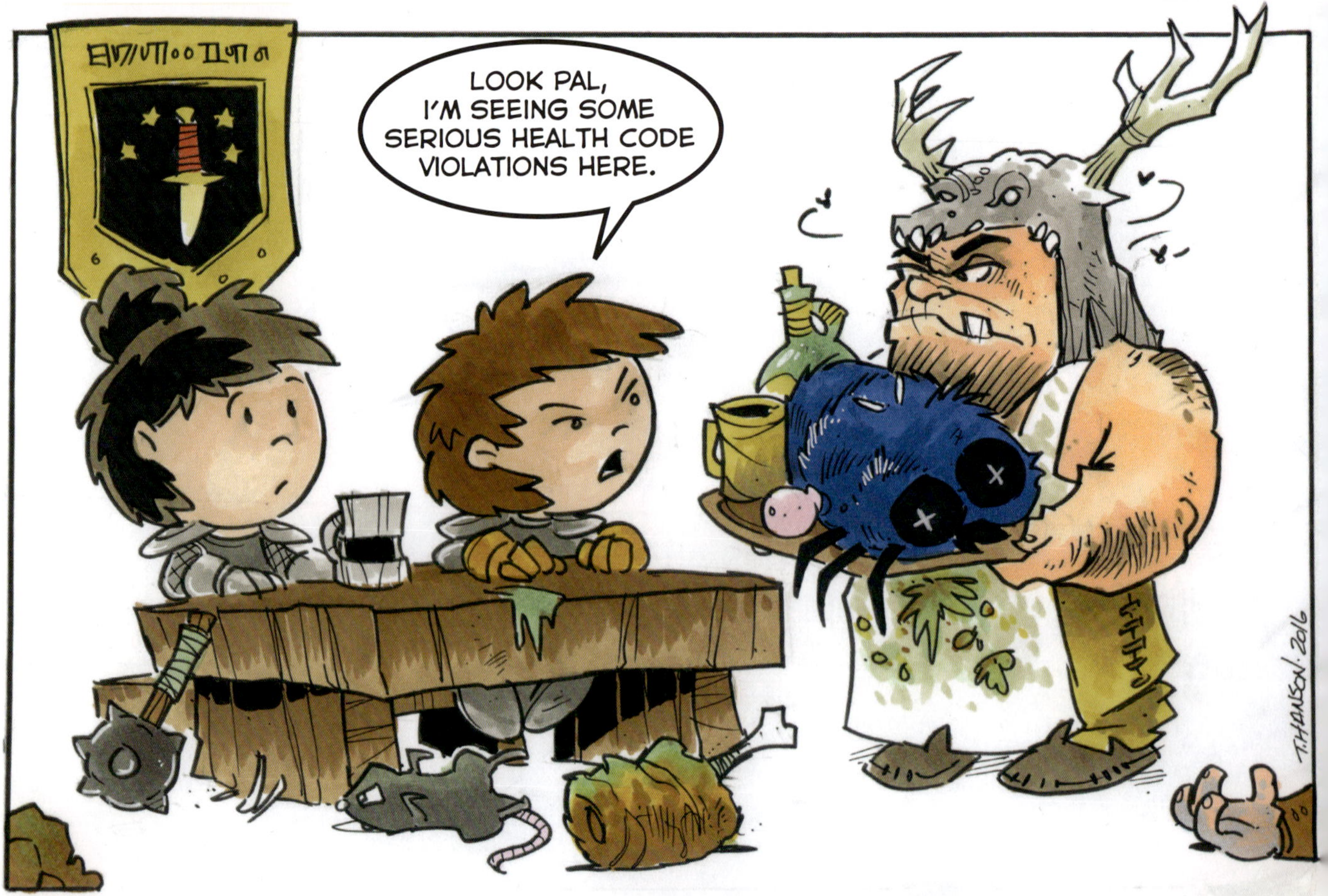

Life of the Party: Realities of an RPG'er
by Travis Hanson

"GOBLIN ARROW ATTACK."

"DRAGON CLAW TO THE GUT."

"PENCIL STAB WOUND BY AN ANGRY GM"

Life of the Party: Realities of an RPG'er

by Travis Hanson

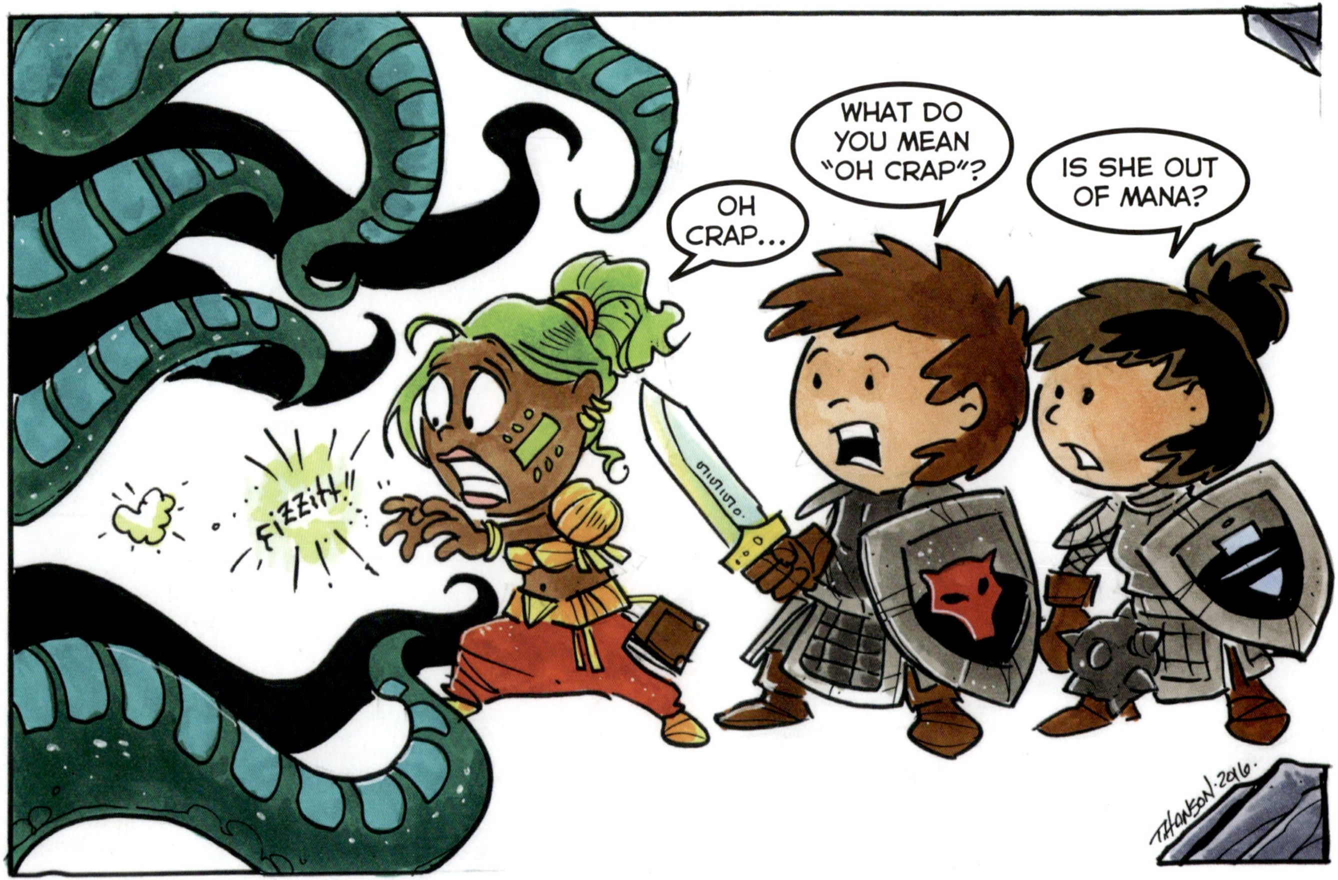

Life of the Party: Realities of an RPG'er

by Travis Hanson

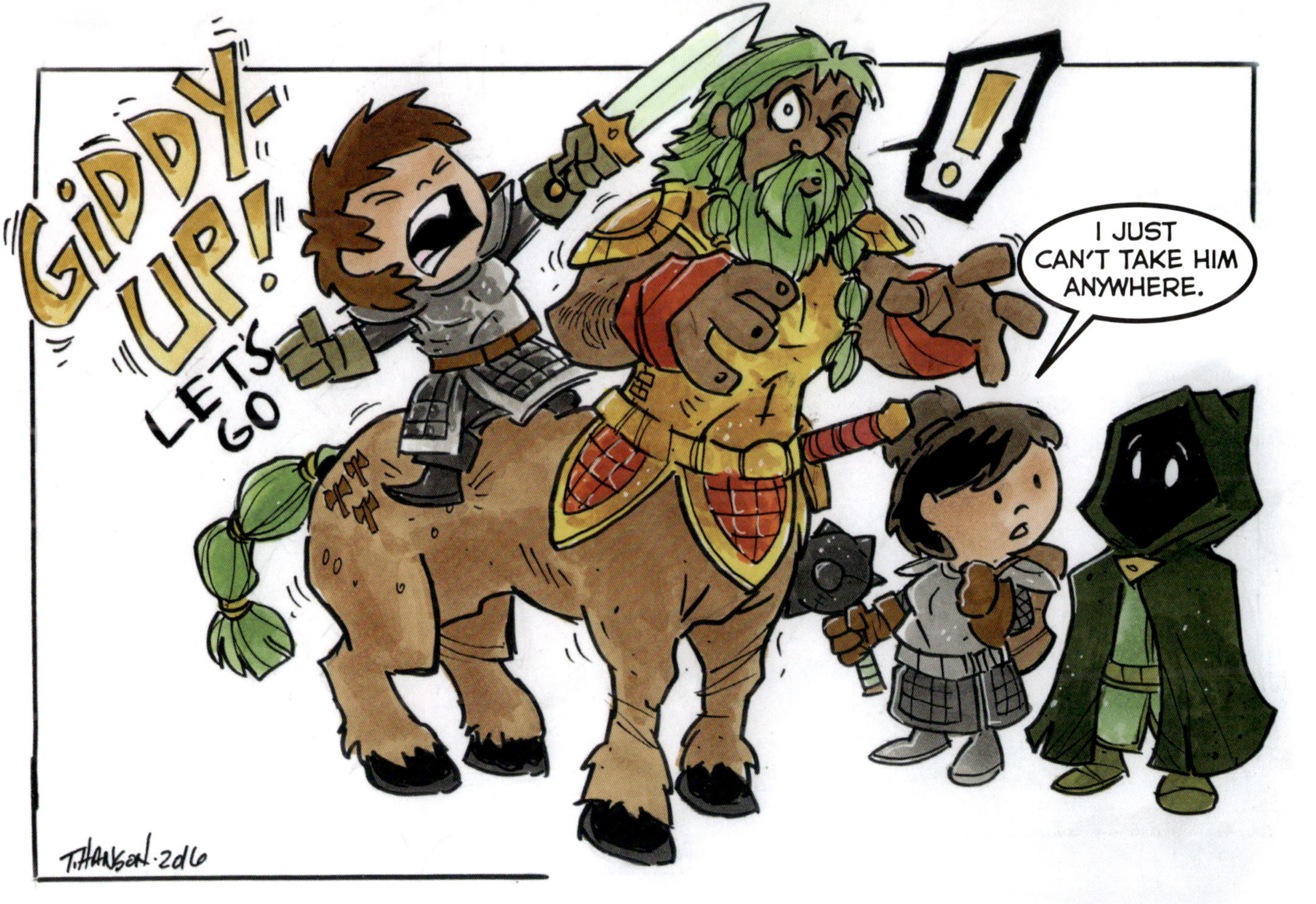

Life of the Party: Realities of an RPG'er by Travis Hanson

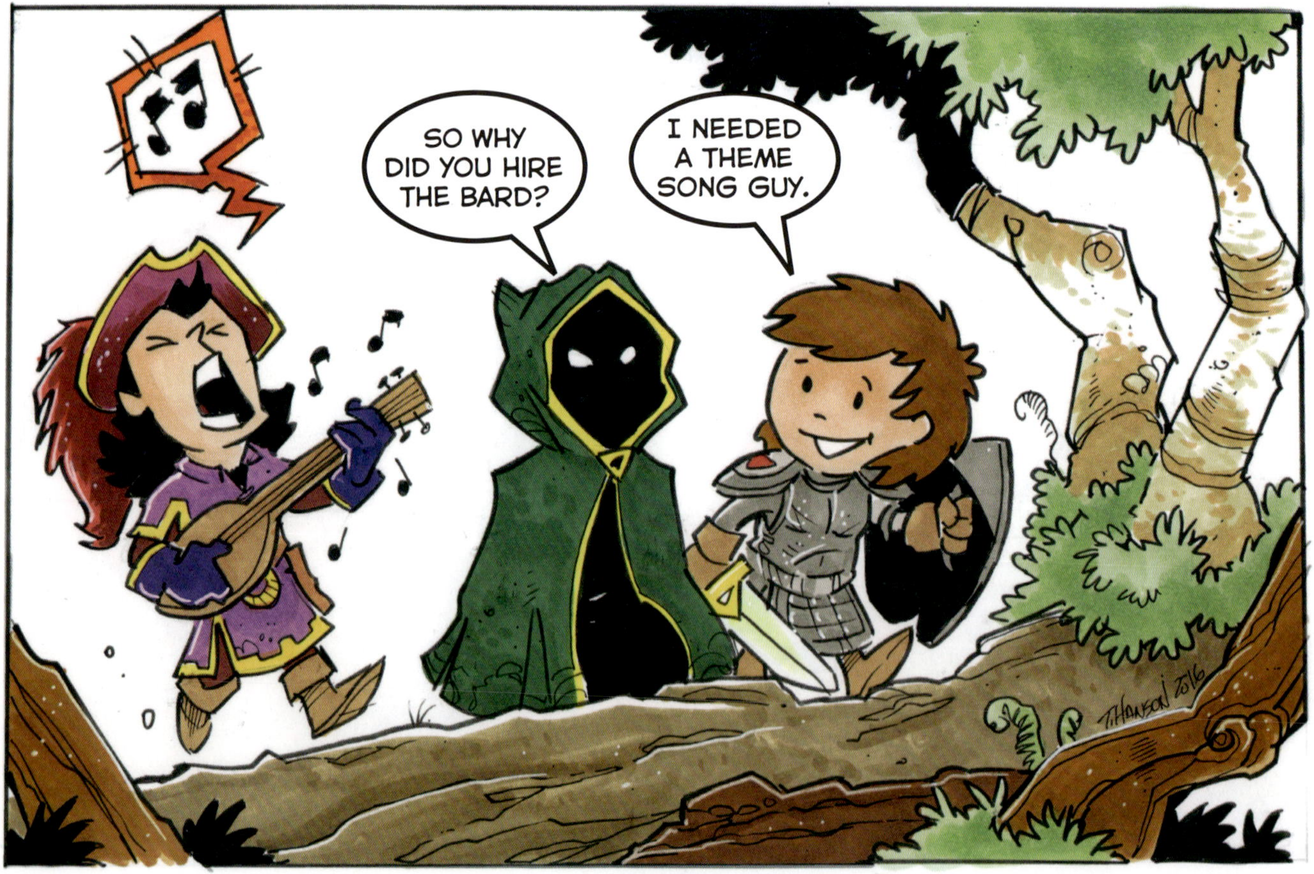

Life of the Party: Realities of an RPG'er by Travis Hanson

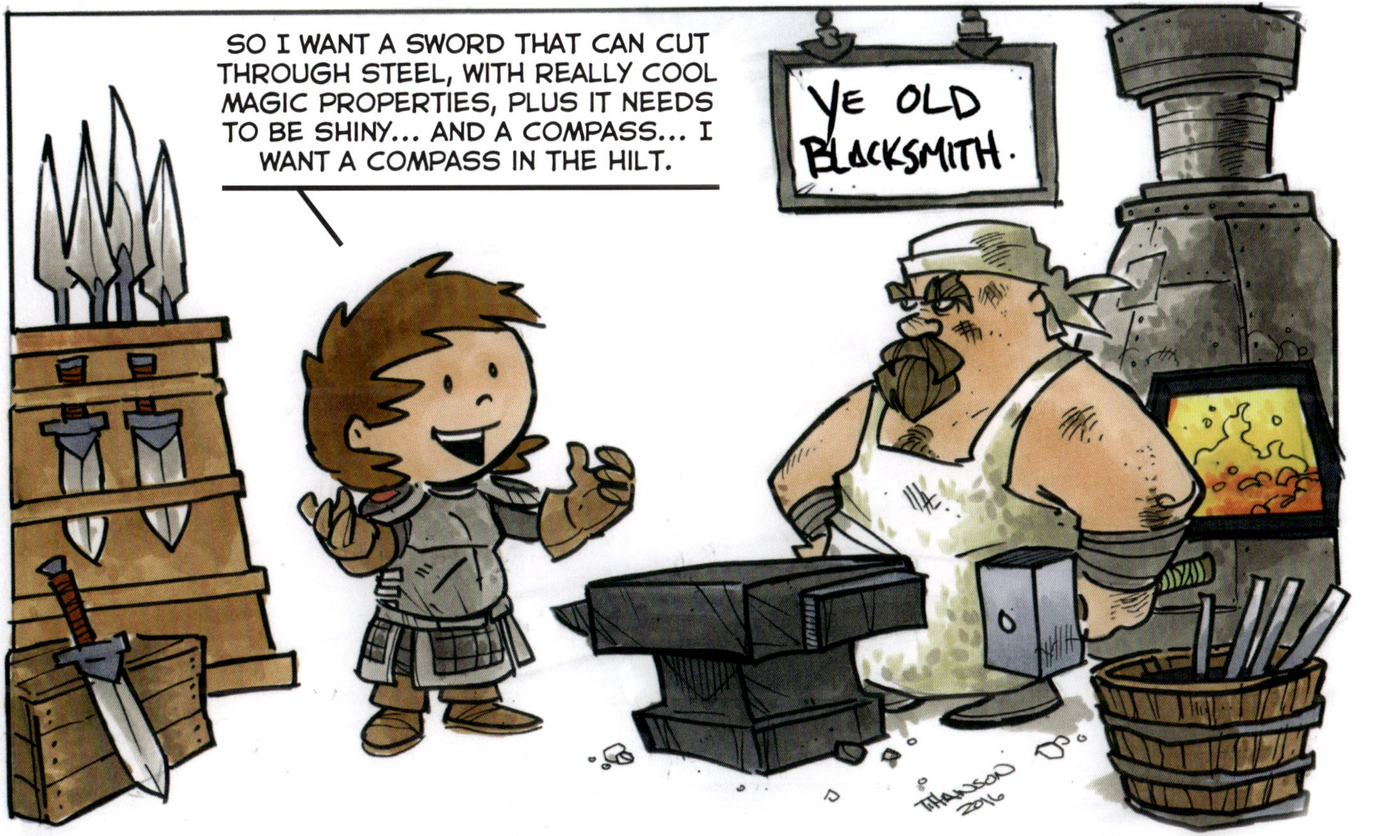

Life of the Party: Realities of an RPG'er
by Travis Hanson

BRING IT ON...

HE'S AS GENTLE AS A LAMB. TRAINED HIM MYSELF SINCE HE WAS JUST A PUP. WOULDN'T HURT A FLY I TELL YOU.
T. HANSON. 2016

Life of the Party: Realities of an RPG'er — by Travis Hanson

Life of the Party: Realities of an RPG'er by Travis Hanson

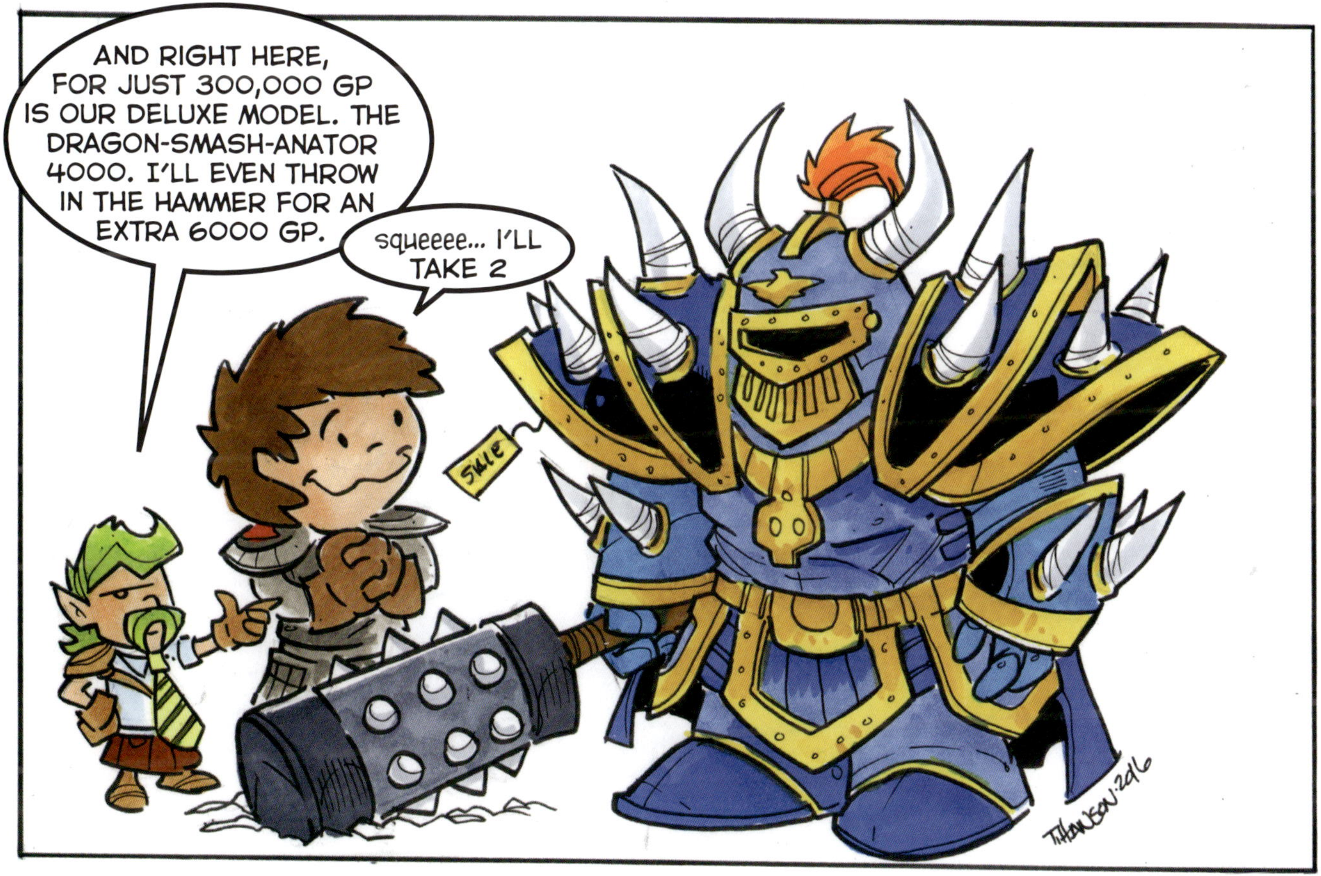

Life of the Party: Realities of an RPG'er

by Travis Hanson

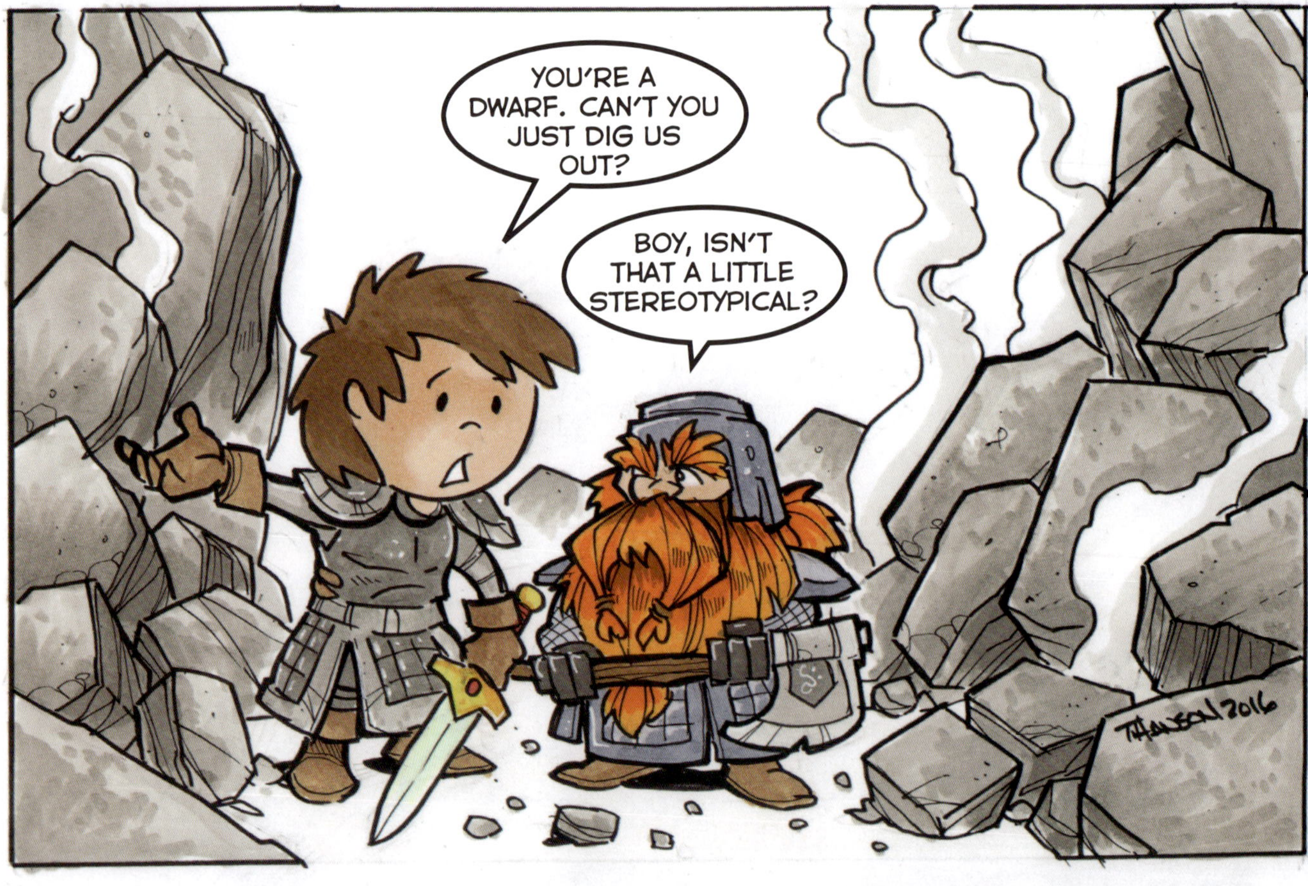

Life of the Party: Realities of an RPG'er

by Travis Hanson

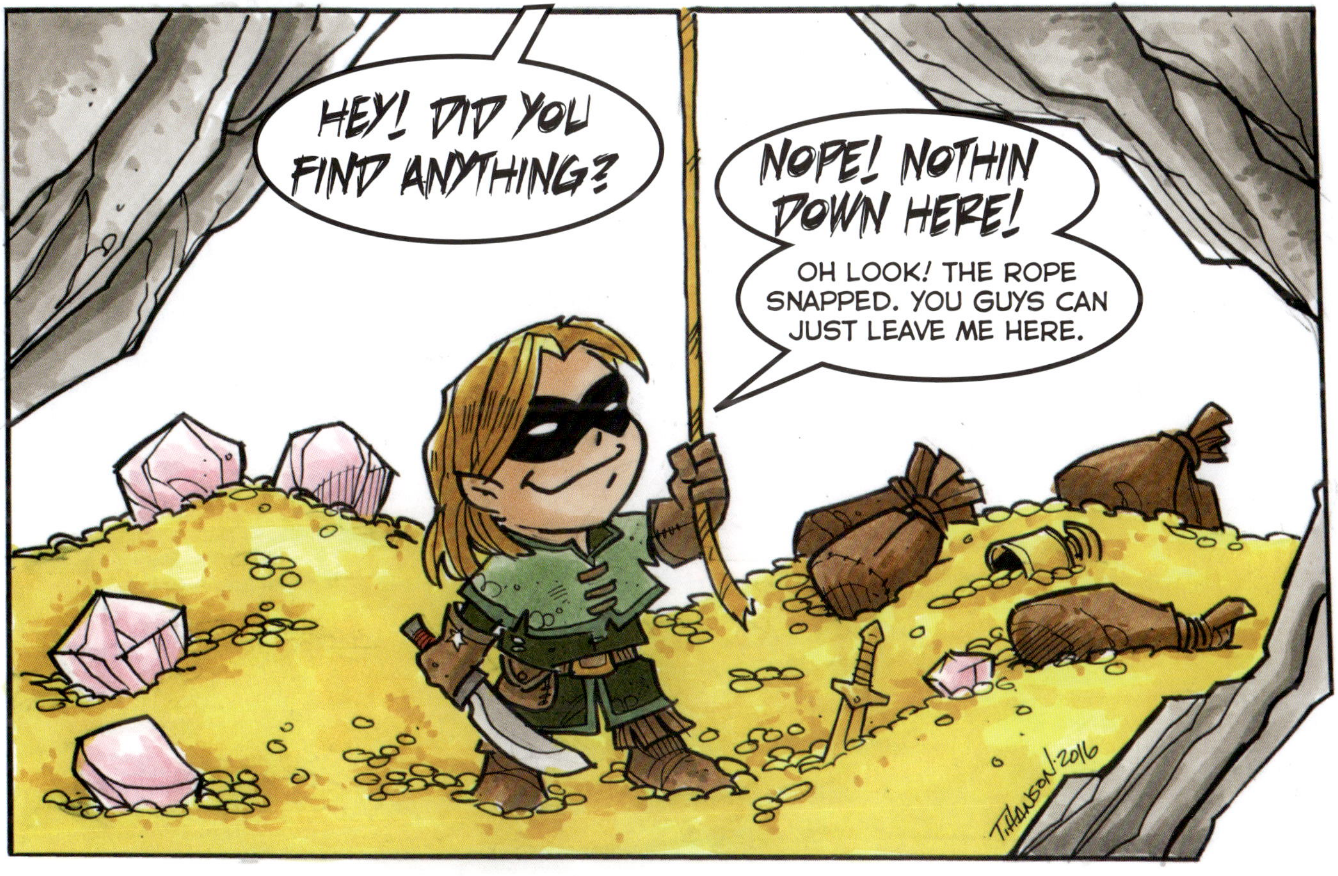

Life of the Party: Realities of an RPG'er
by Travis Hanson

Life of the Party: Realities of an RPG'er

by Travis Hanson

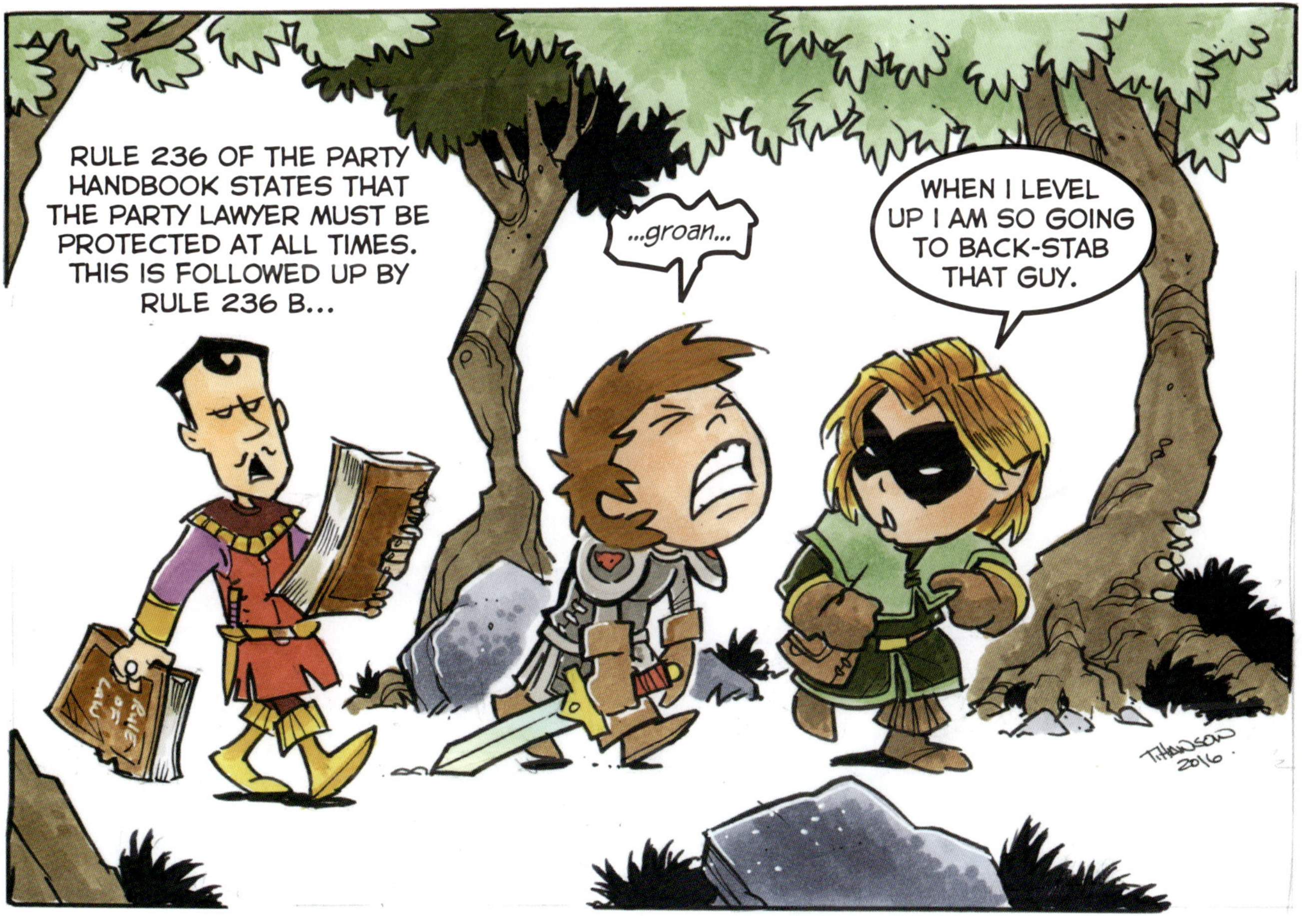

Life of the Party: Realities of an RPG'er

by Travis Hanson

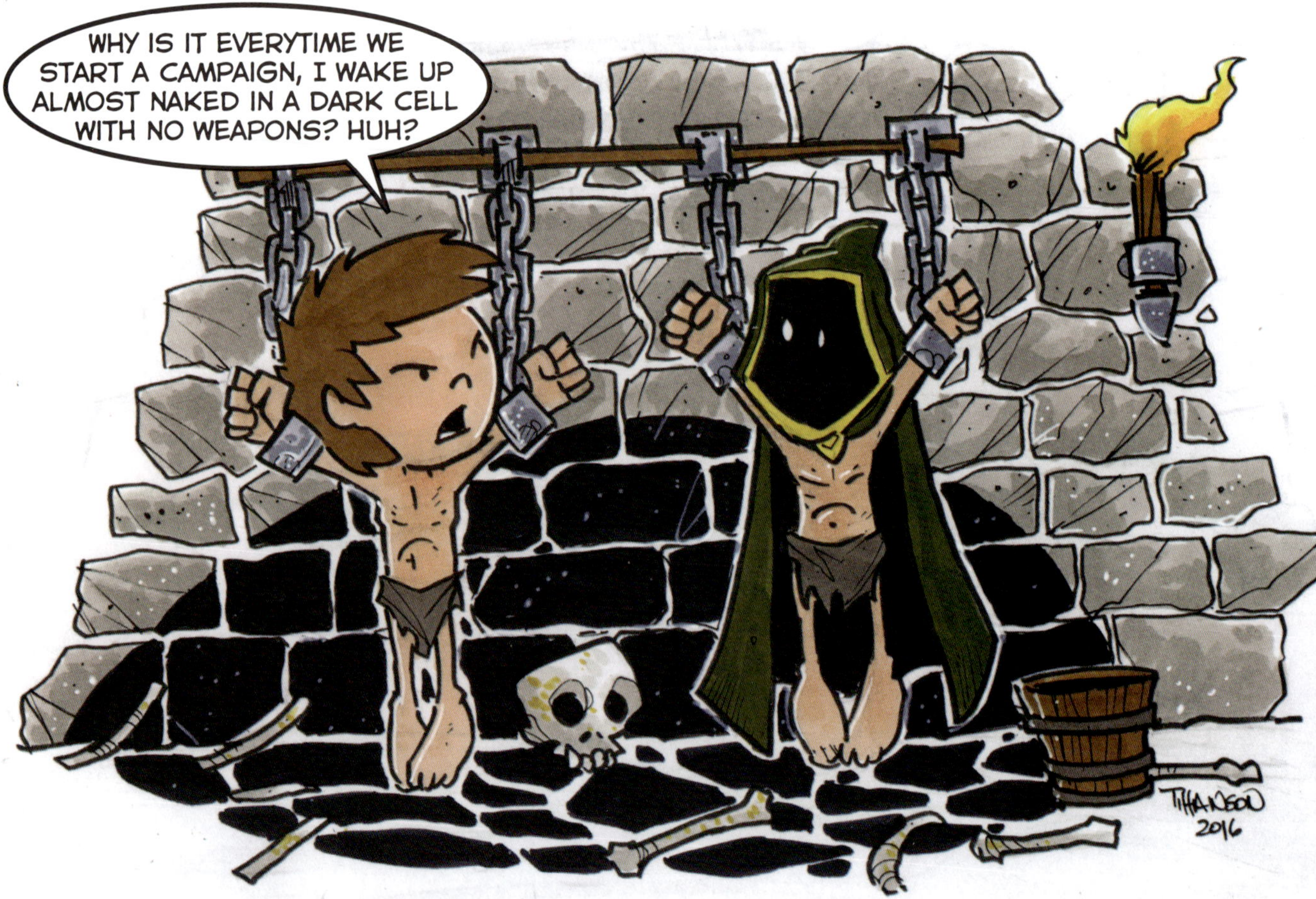

Life of the Party: Realities of an RPG'er

by Travis Hanson

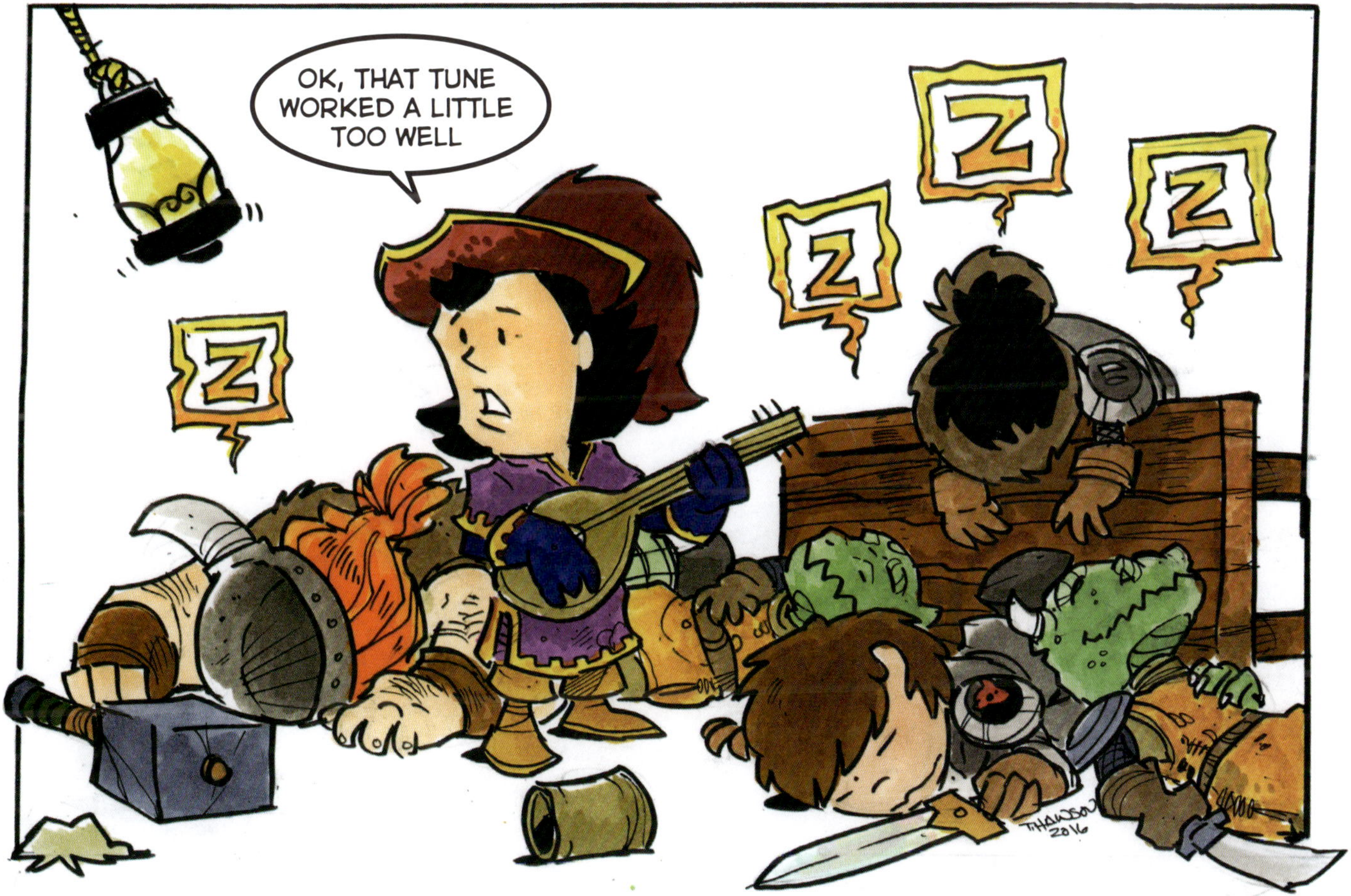

Life of the Party: Realities of an RPG'er

by Travis Hanson

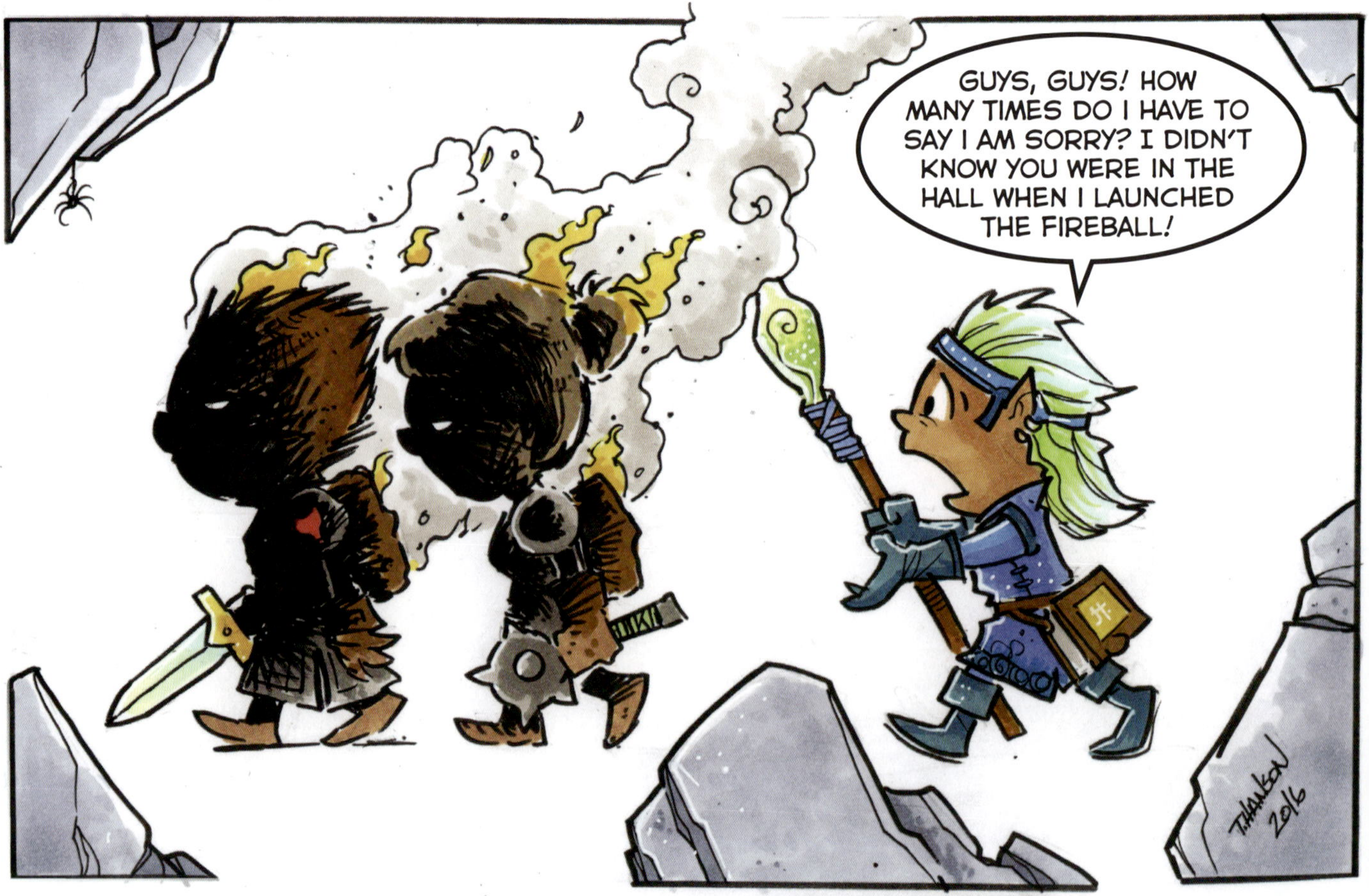

Life of the Party: Realities of an RPG'er

by Travis Hanson

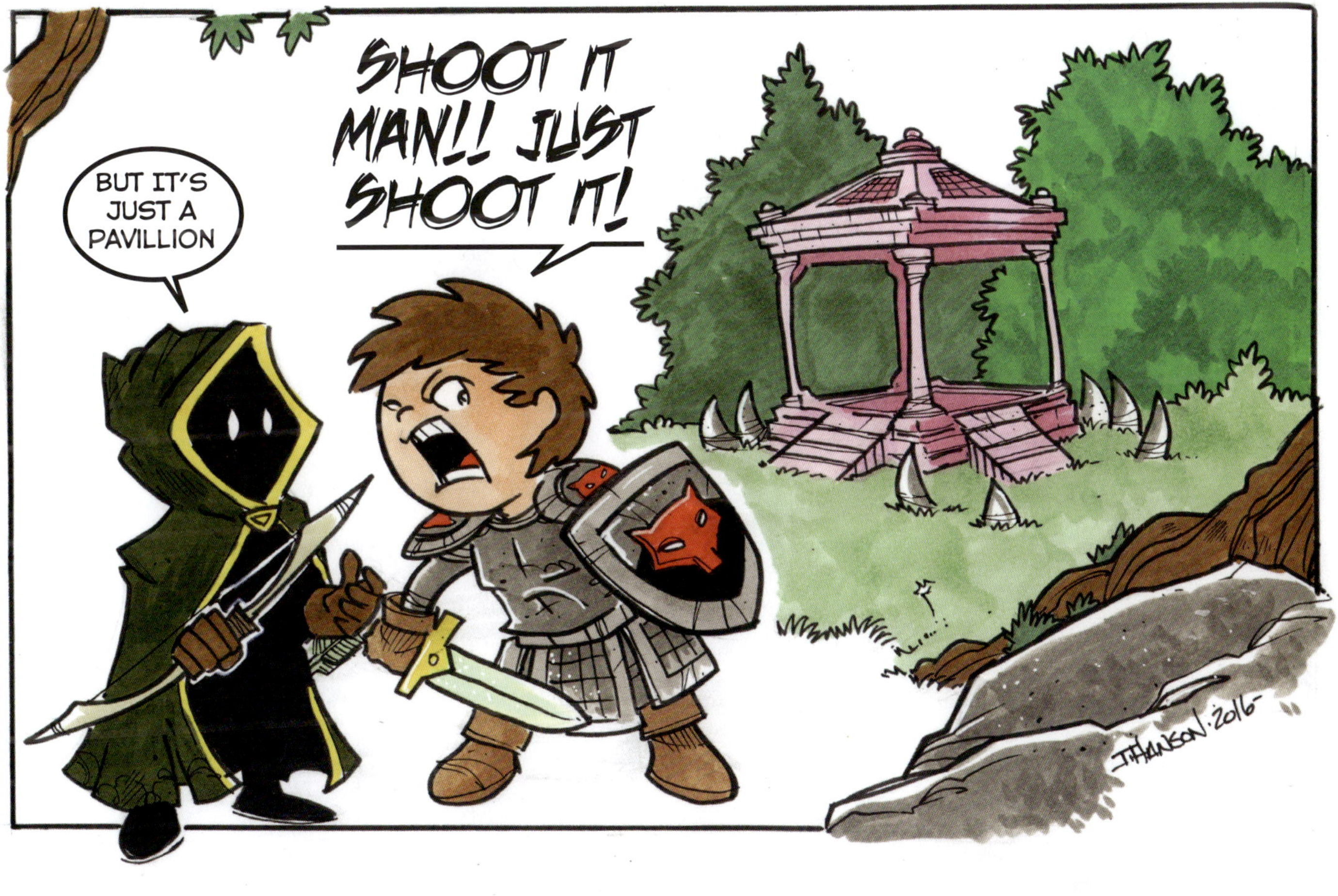

Life of the Party: Realities of an RPG'er by Travis Hanson

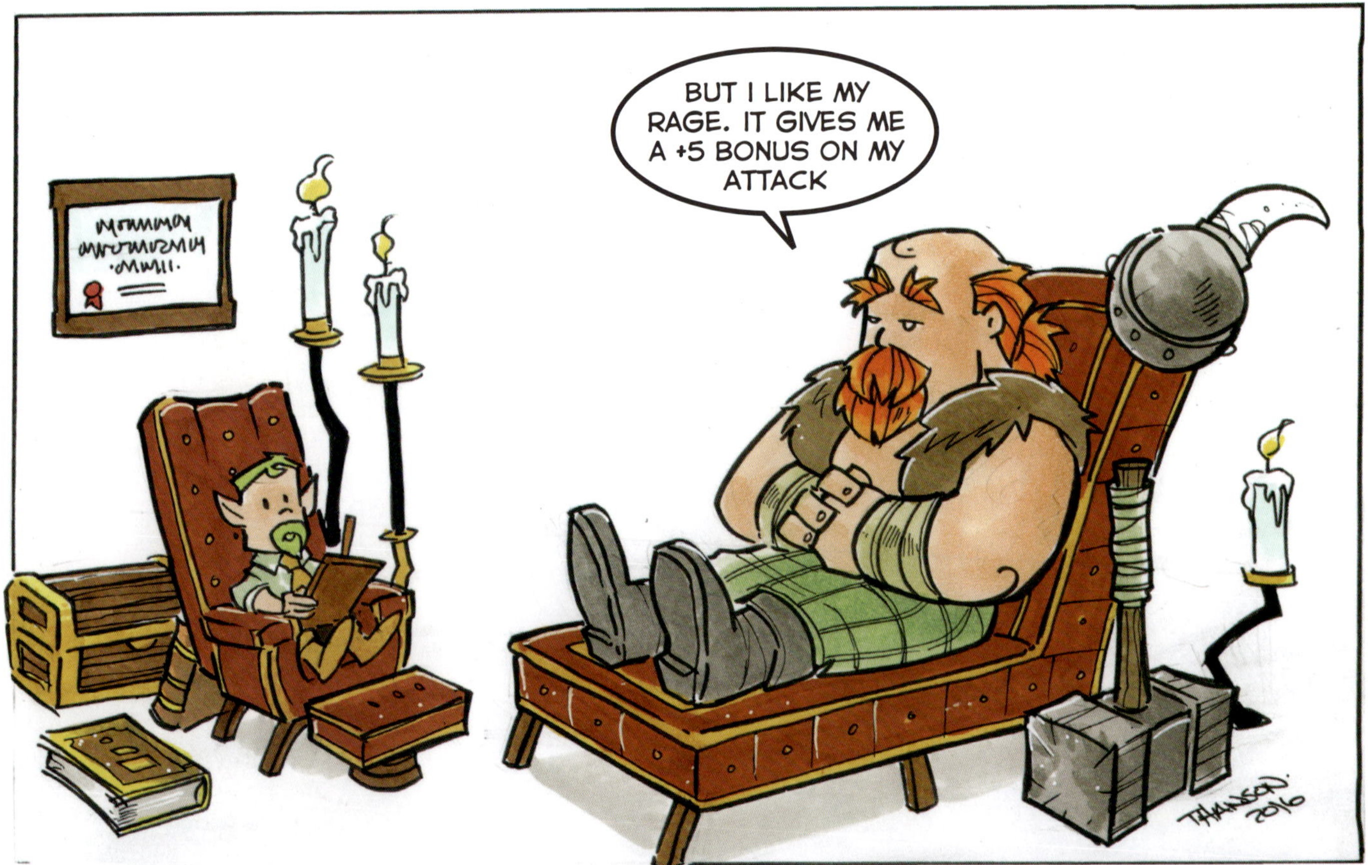

Life of the Party: Realities of an RPG'er

by Travis Hanson

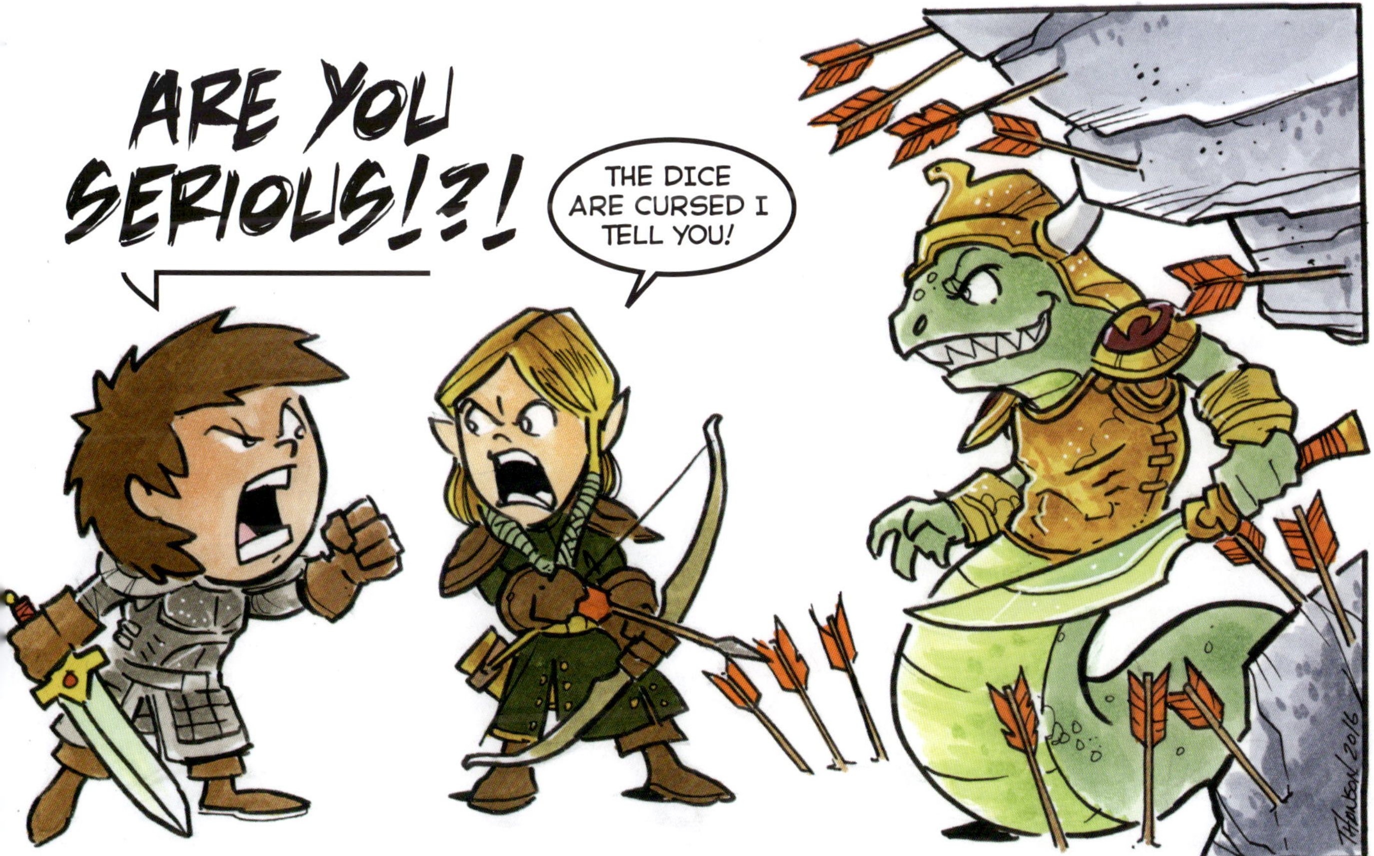

by Travis Hanson

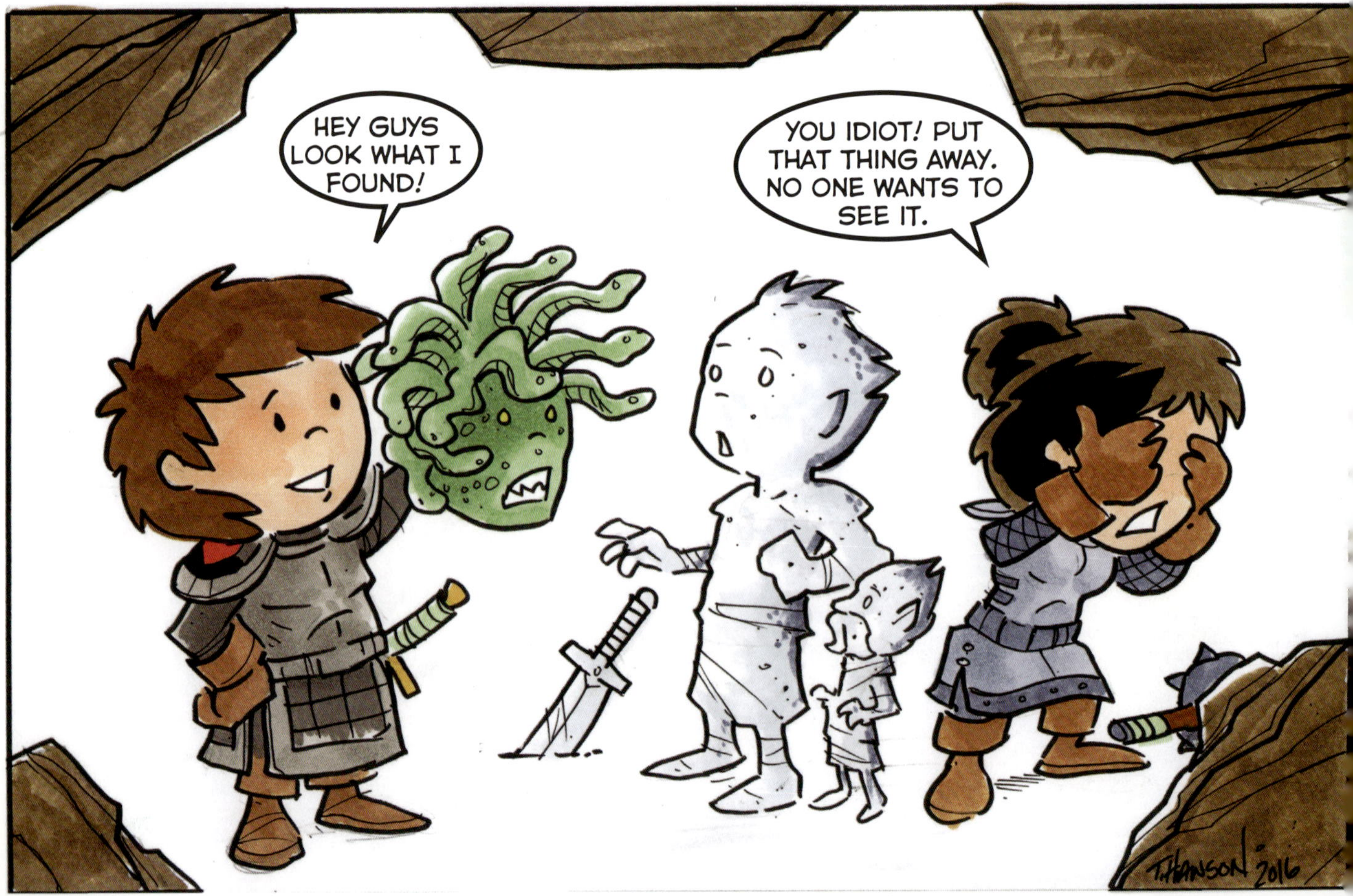

Life of the Party: Realities of an RPG'er

by Travis Hanson

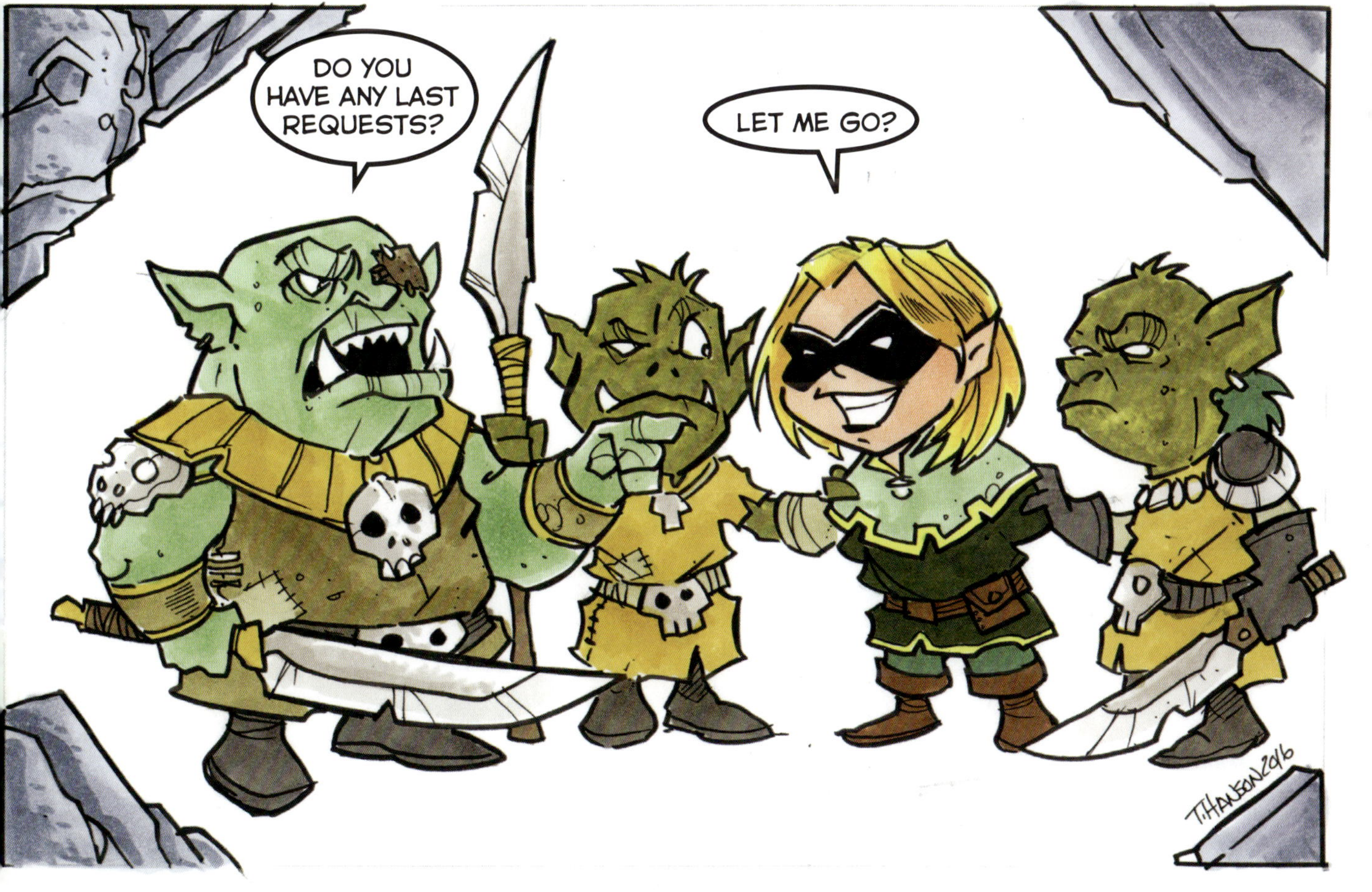

Life of the Party: Realities of an RPG'er

by Travis Hanson

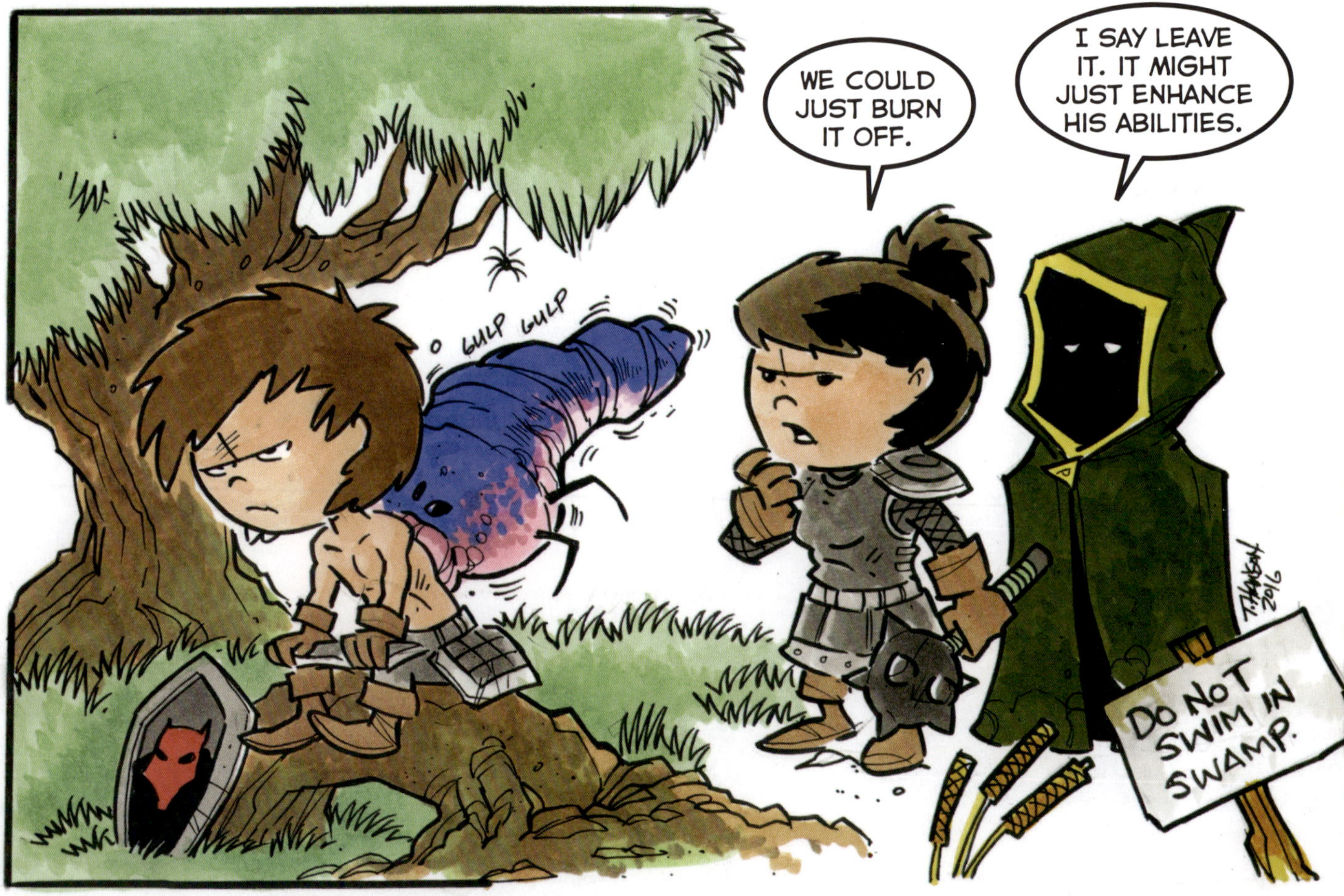

Life of the Party: Realities of an RPG'er

by Travis Hanson

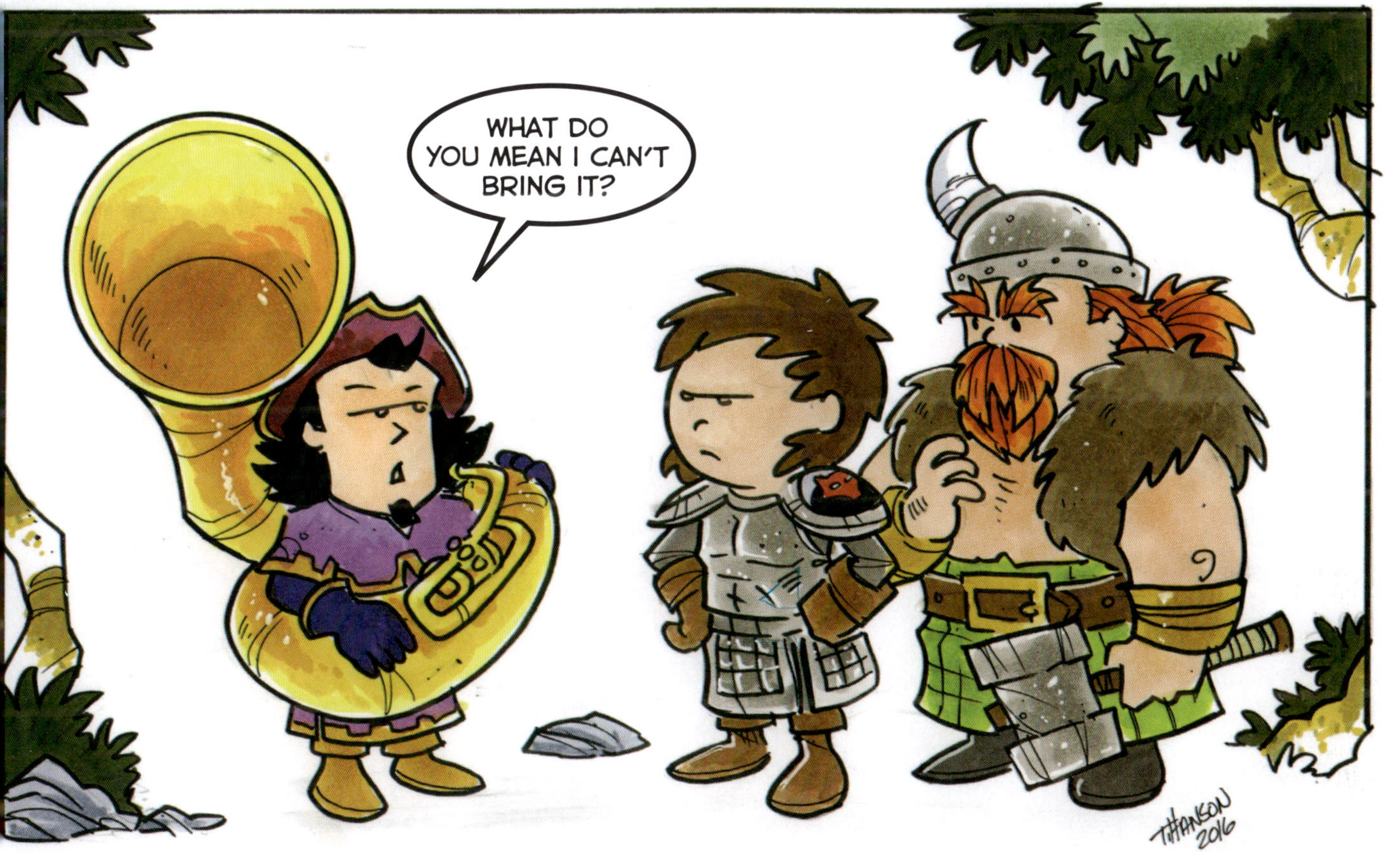

THAT WAS MY FAVORITE SWORD AND ARMOR!!
OH STOP YOUR WHINING!
T. HANSON 2016

Life of the Party: Realities of an RPG'er

by Travis Hanson

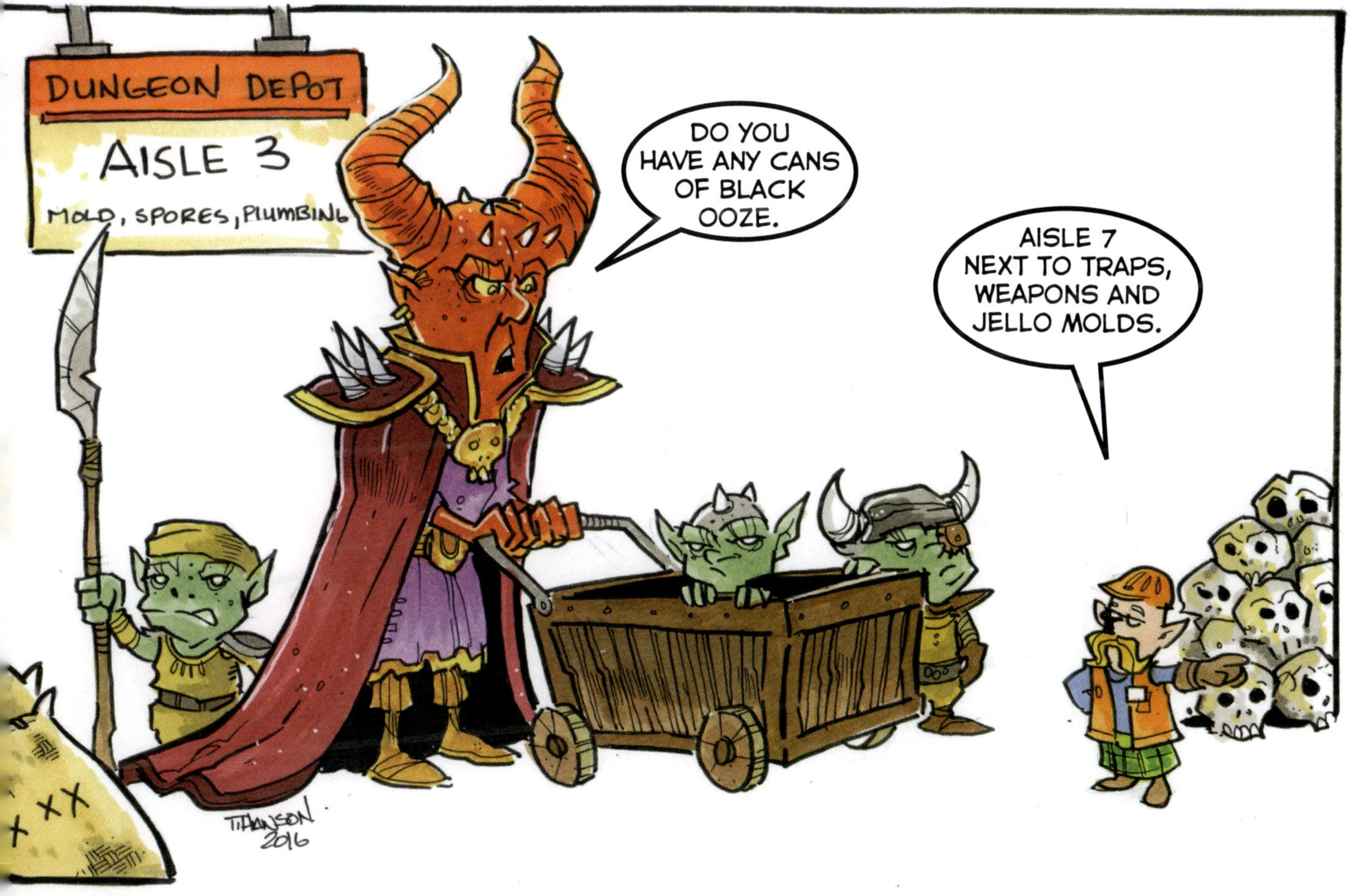

Life of the Party: Realities of an RPG'er

by Travis Hanson

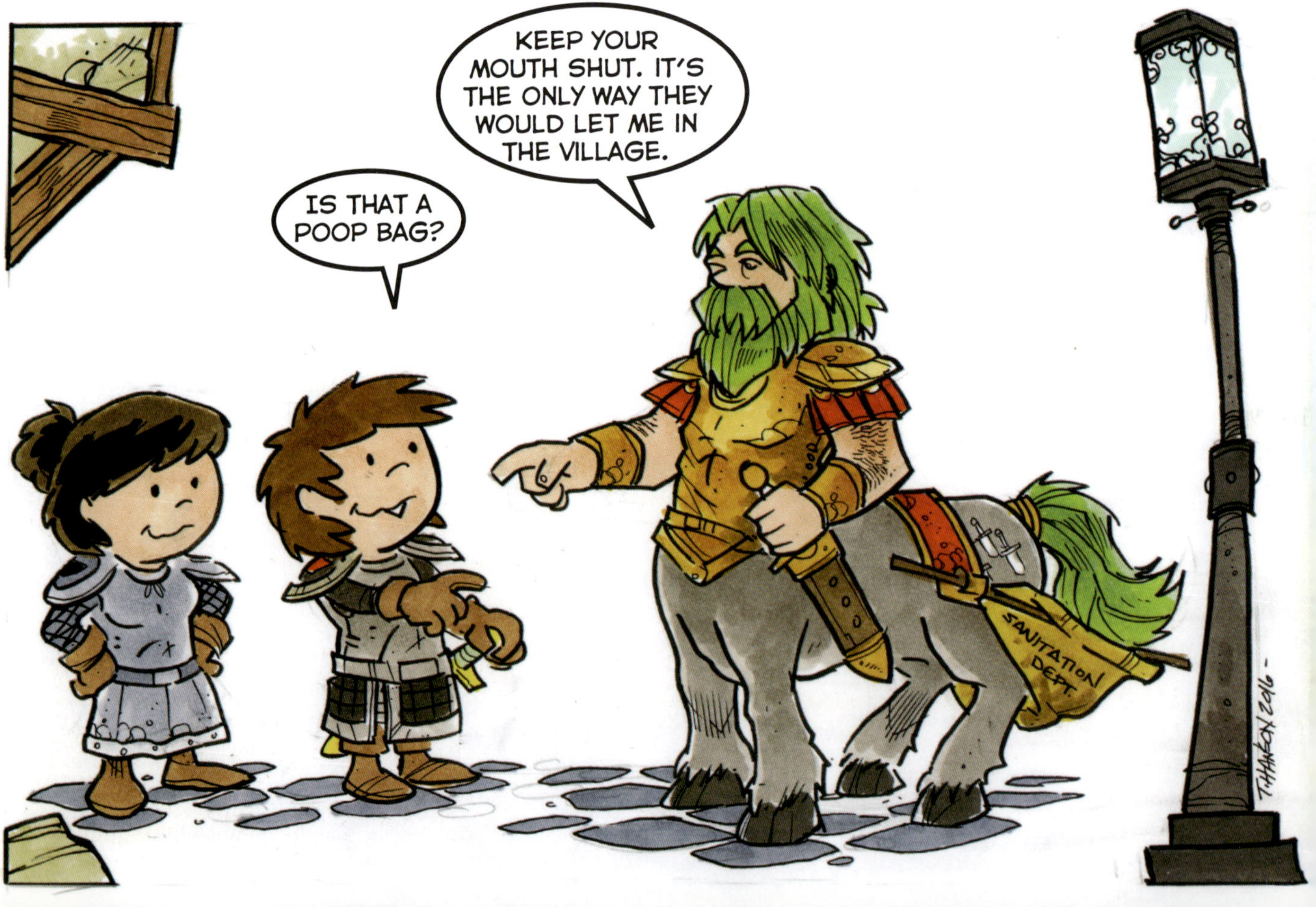

Life of the Party: Realities of an RPG'er

by Travis Hanson

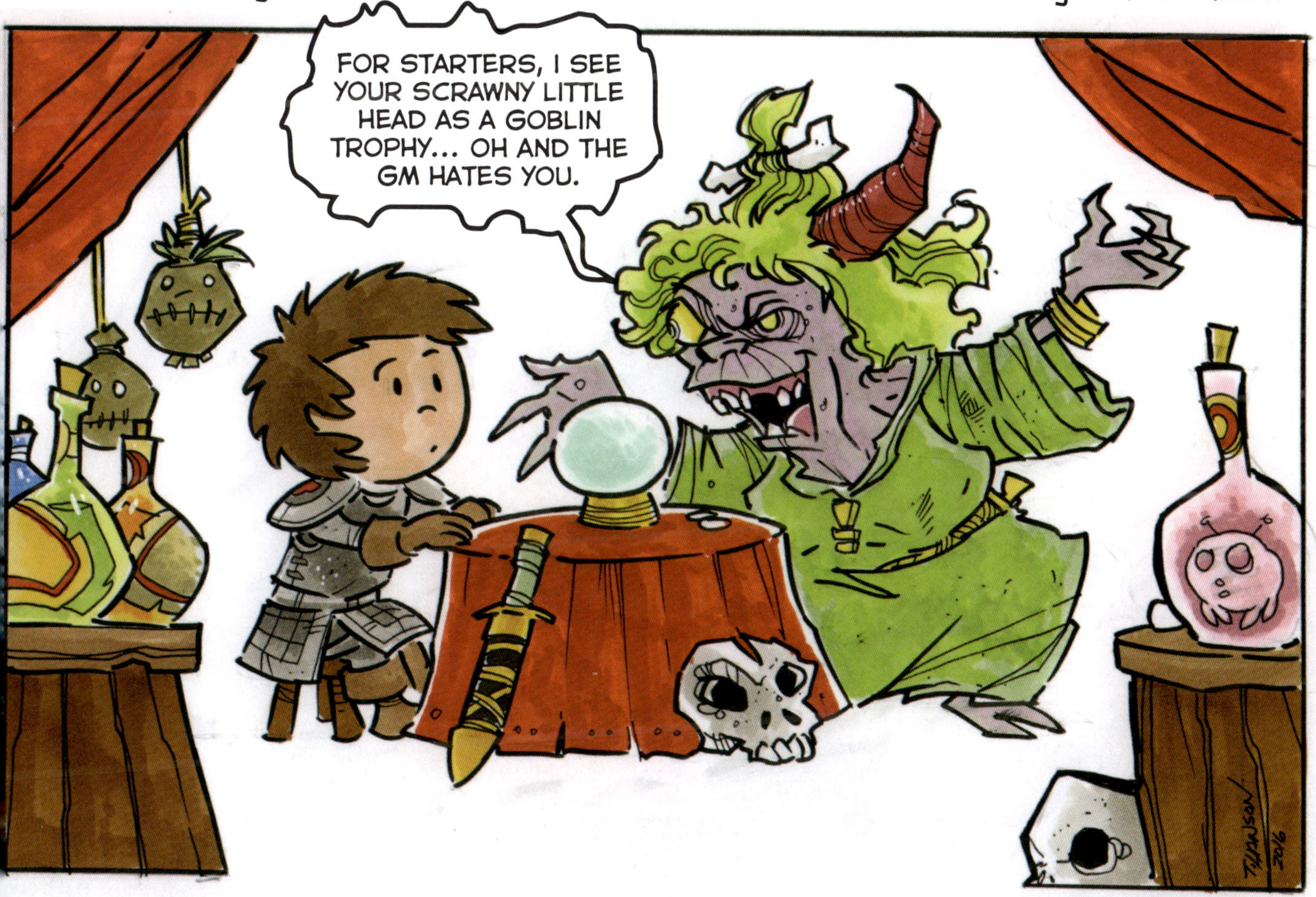

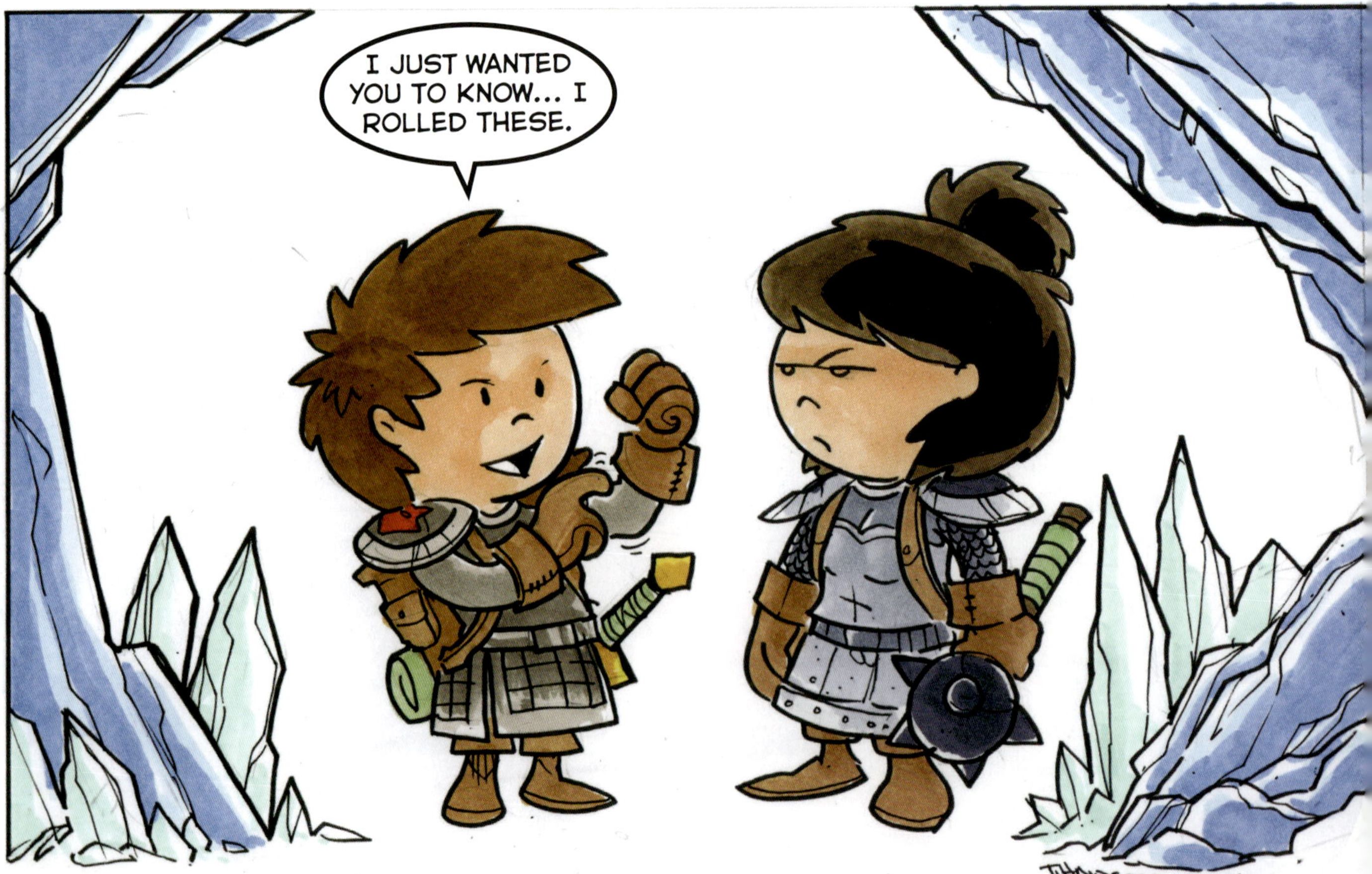

Life of the Party: Realities of an RPG'er

by Travis Hanson

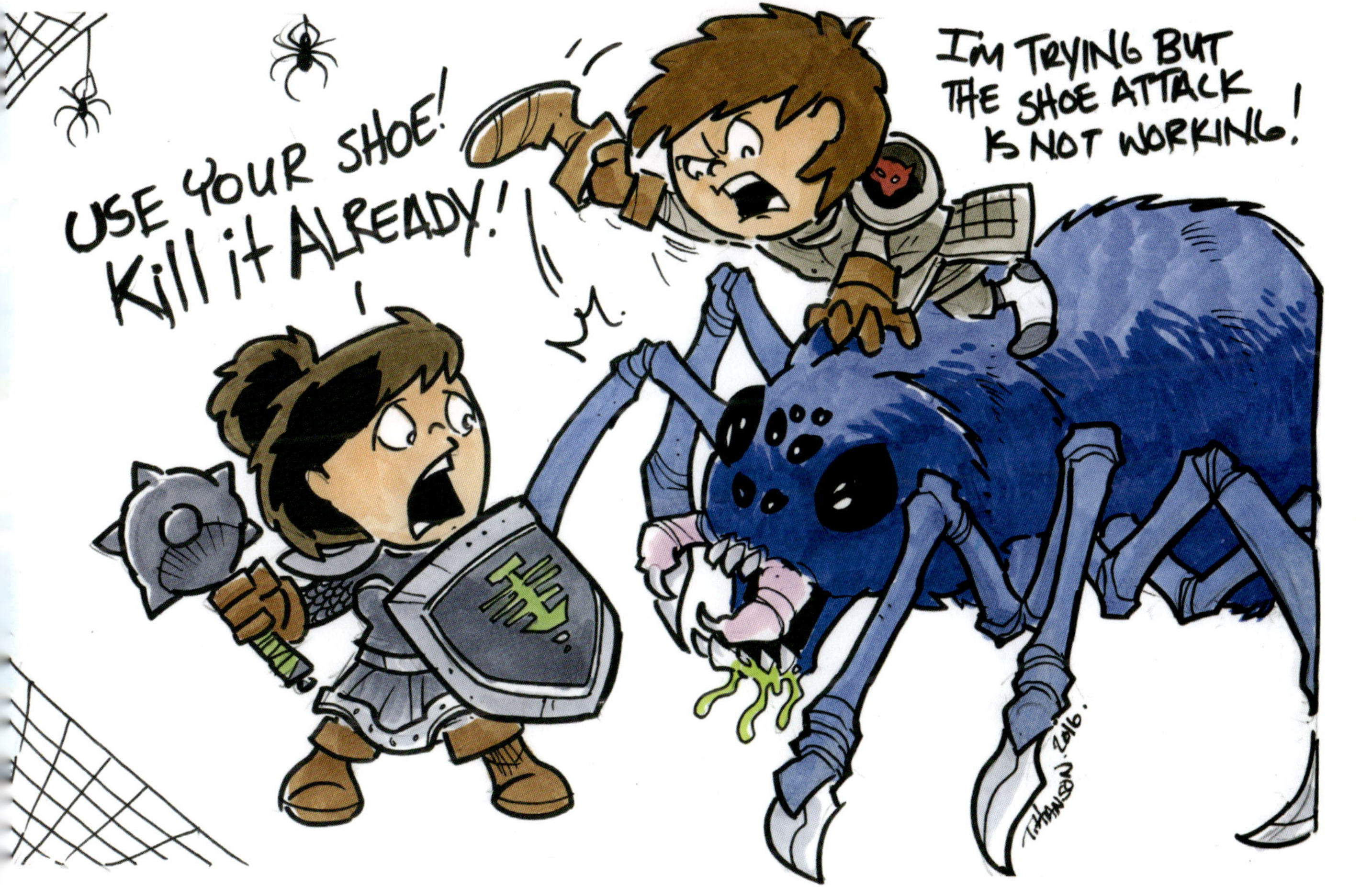

Life of the Party: Realities of an RPG'er by Travis Hanson

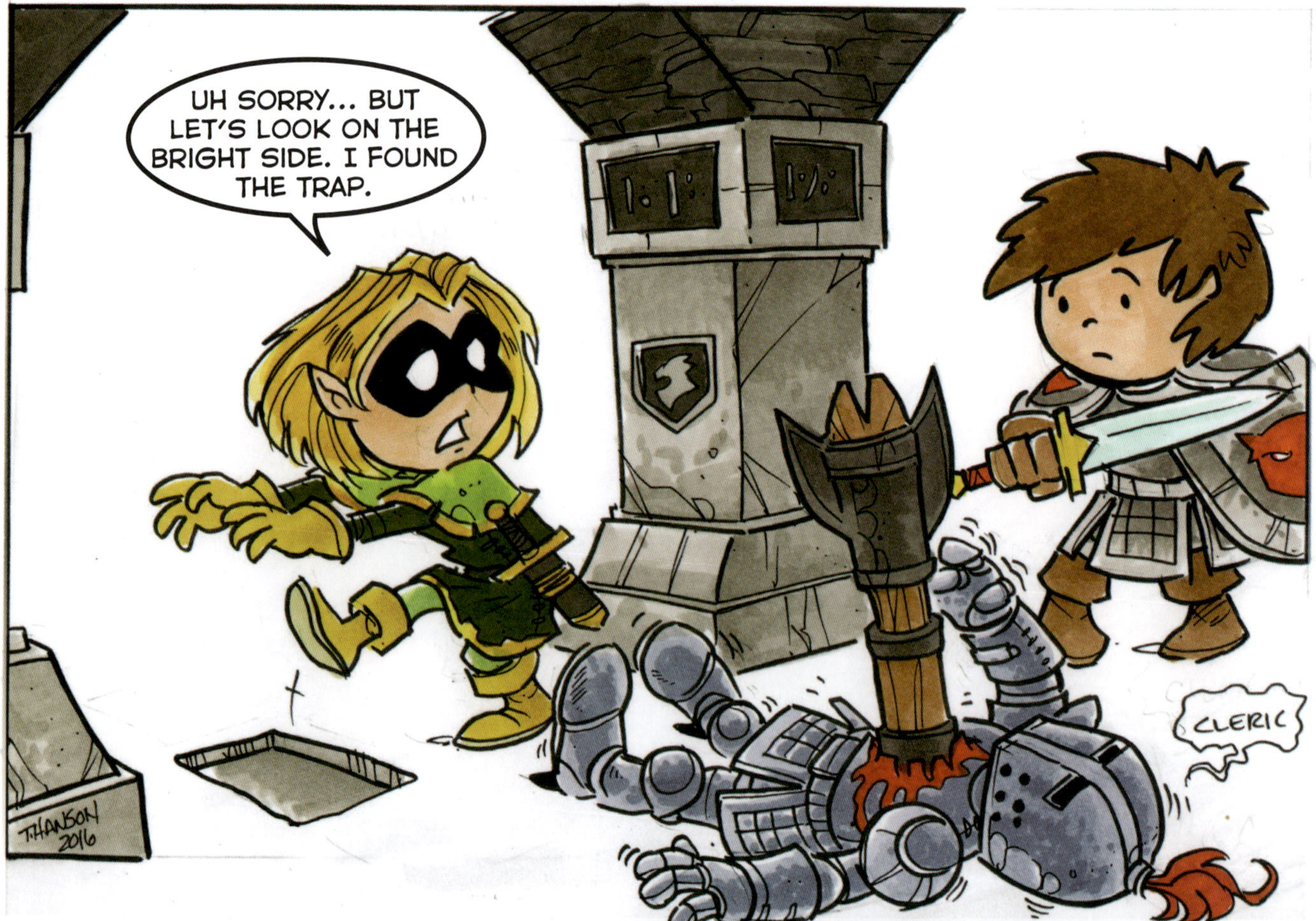

Life of the Party: Realities of an RPG'er

by Travis Hanson

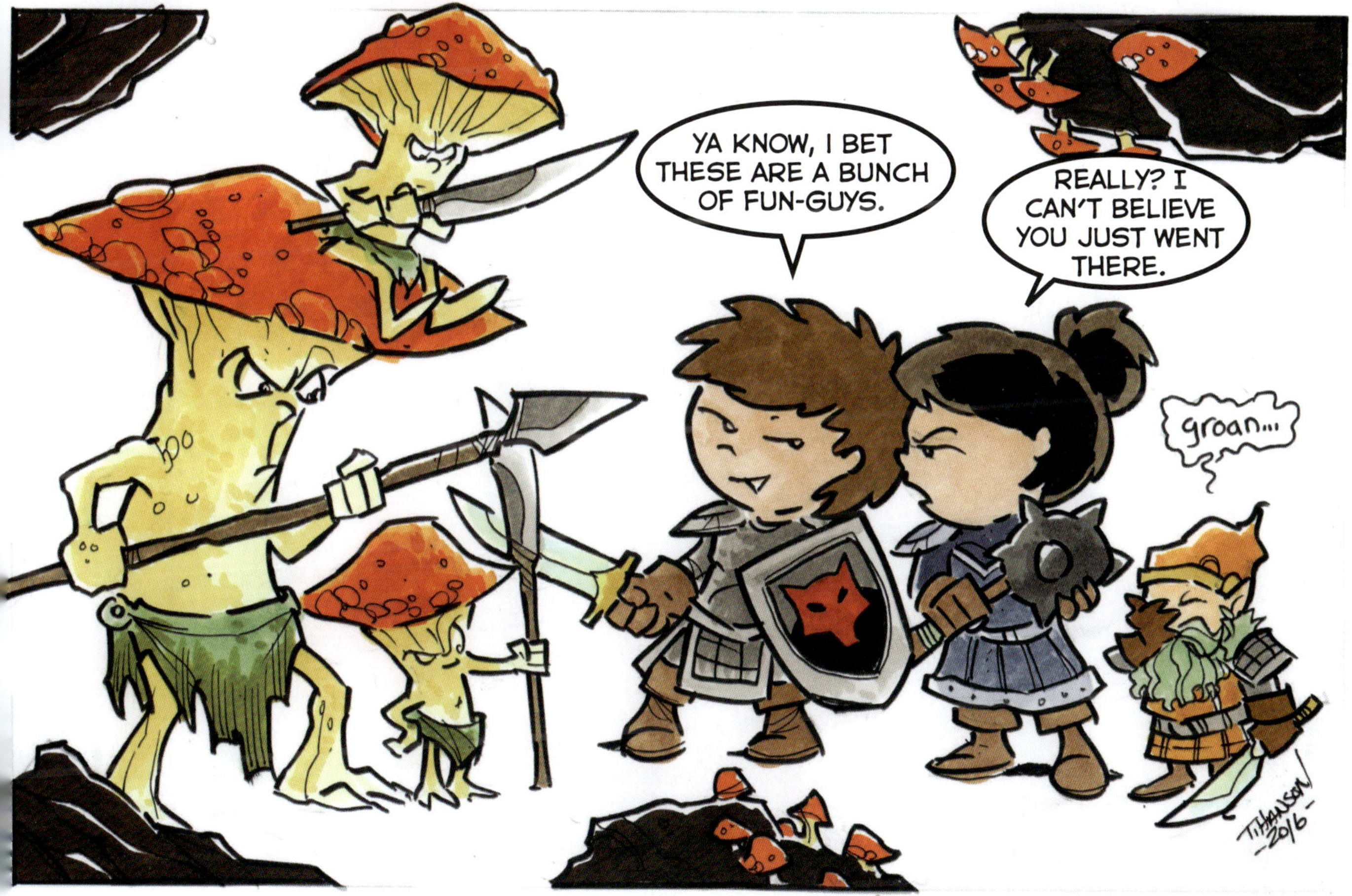

Life of the Party: Realities of an RPG'er

by Travis Hanson

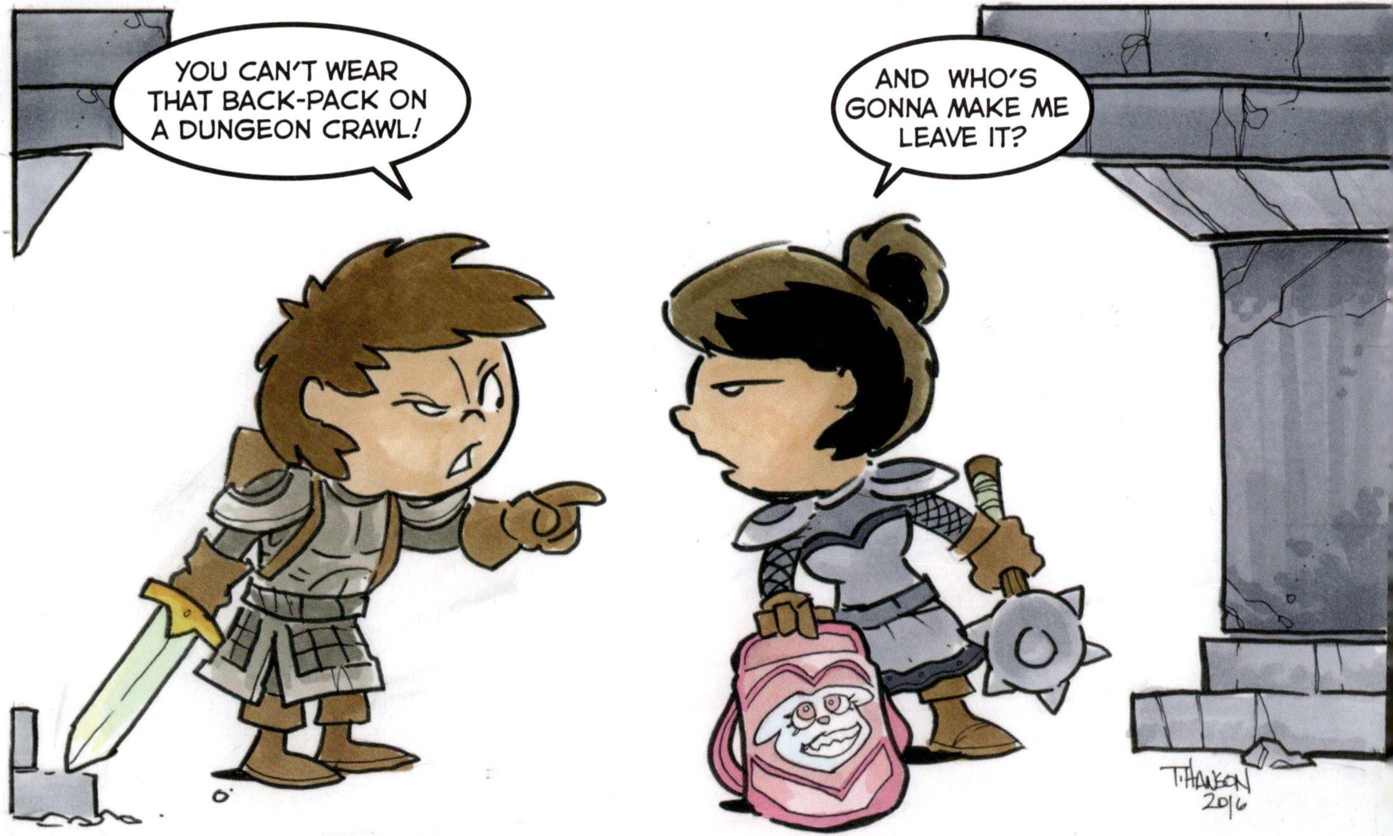

Life of the Party: Realities of an RPG'er — by Travis Hanson

"A LITTLE HELP HERE?"

Life of the Party: Realities of an RPG'er by Travis Hanson

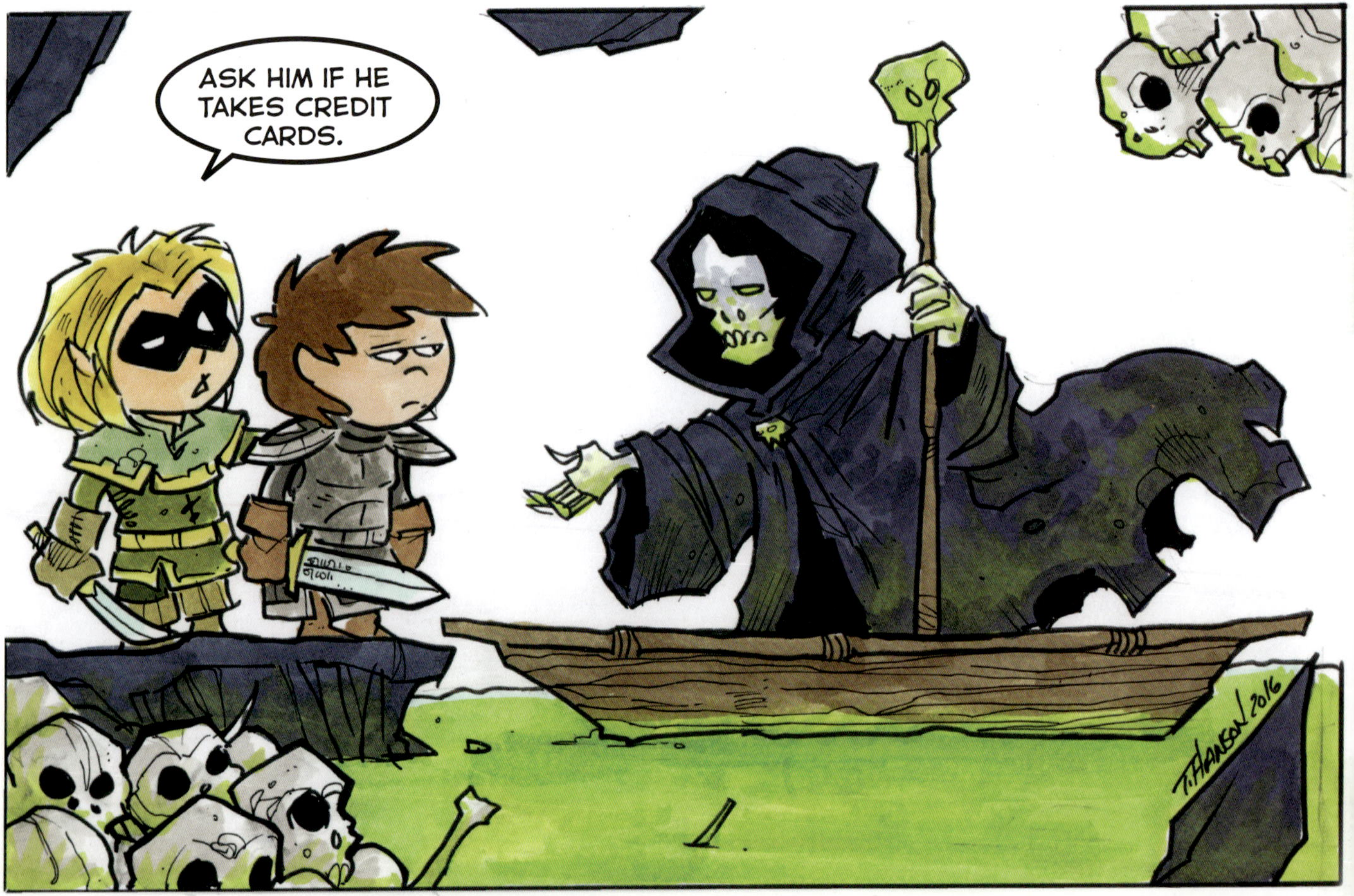

Life of the Party: Realities of an RPG'er

by Travis Hanson

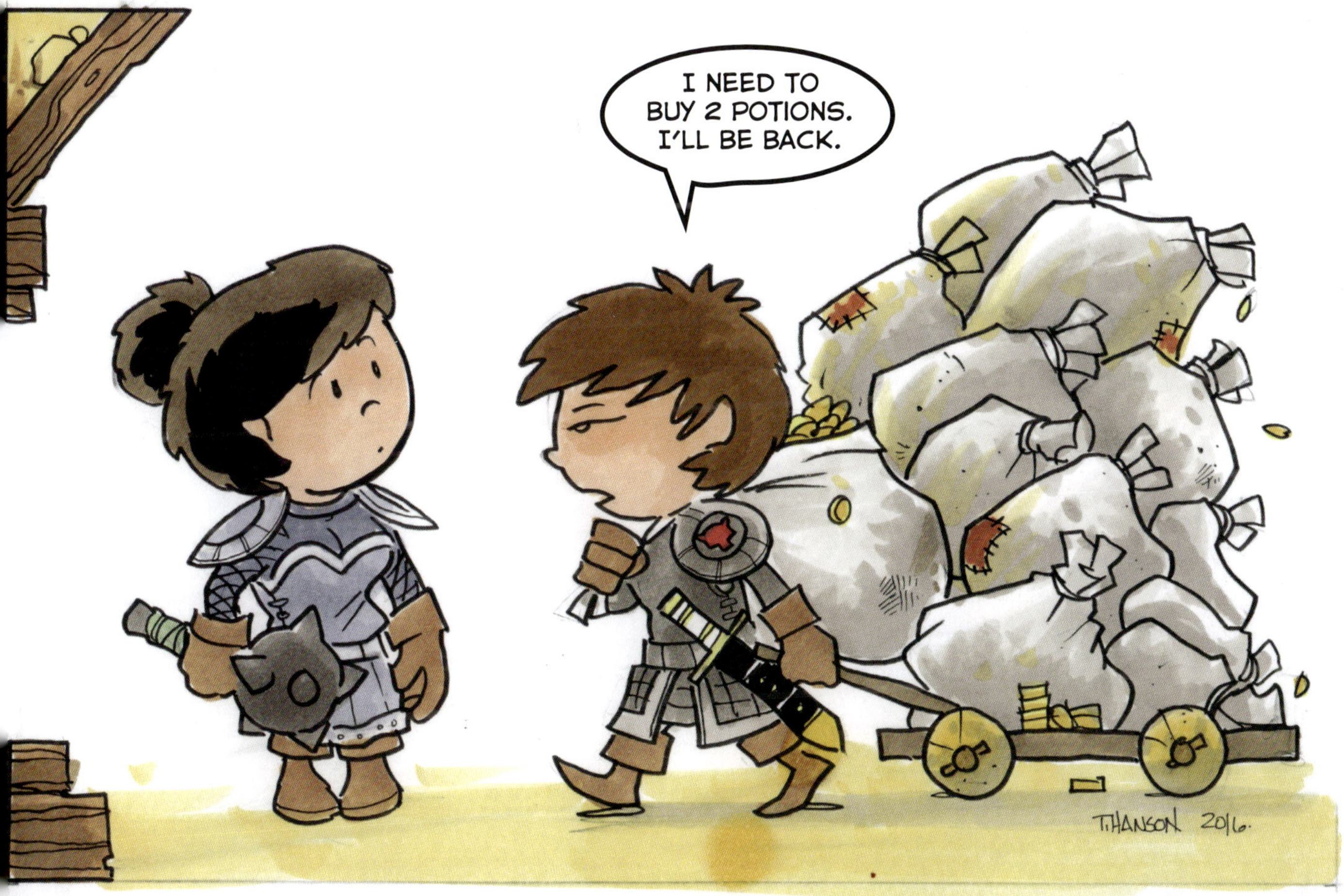

Life of the Party: Realities of an RPG'er

by Travis Hanson

Life of the Party: Realities of an RPG'er — by Travis Hanson

Life of the Party: Realities of an RPG'er

by Travis Hanson

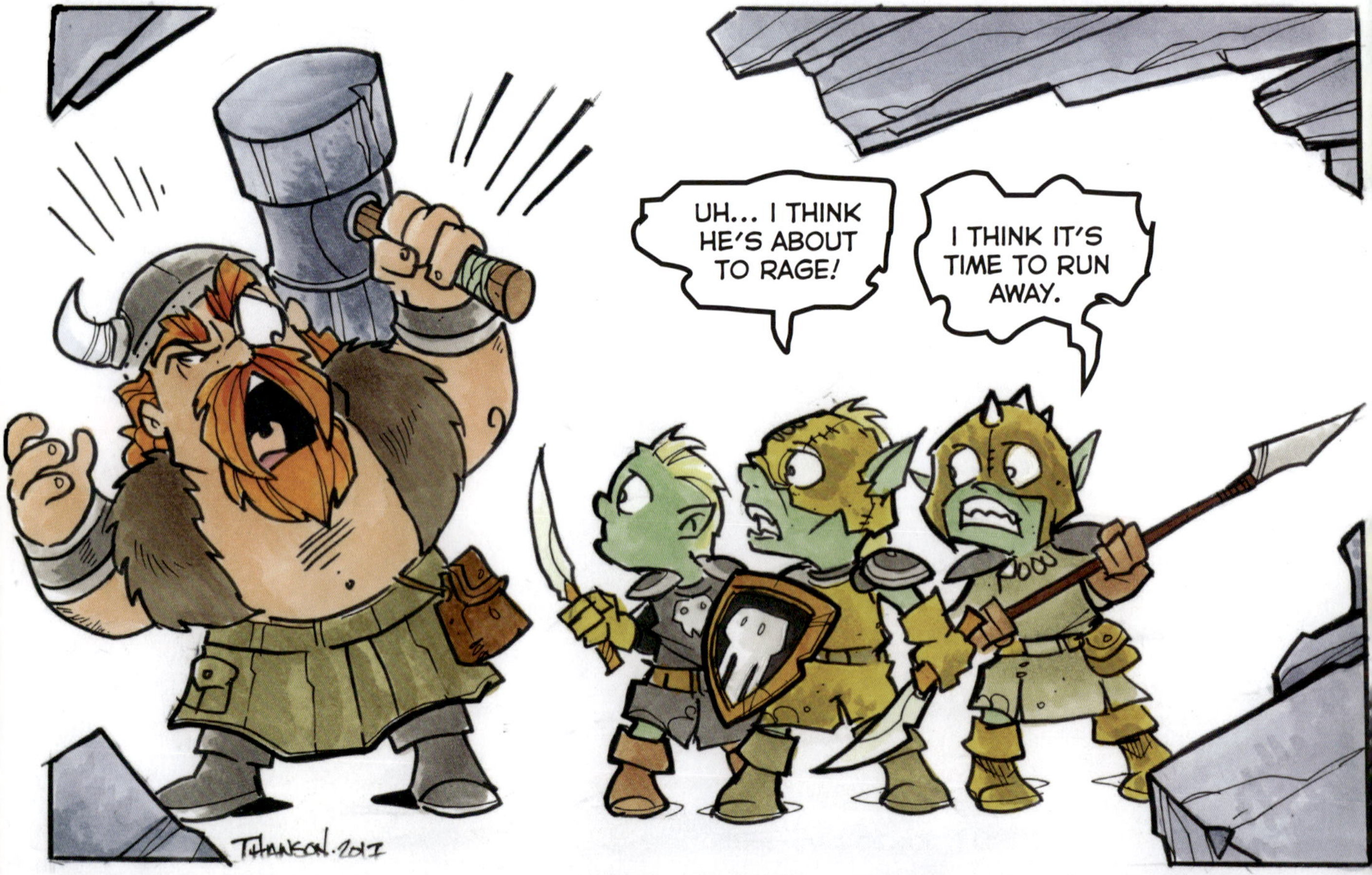

Life of the Party: Realities of an RPG'er by Travis Hanson

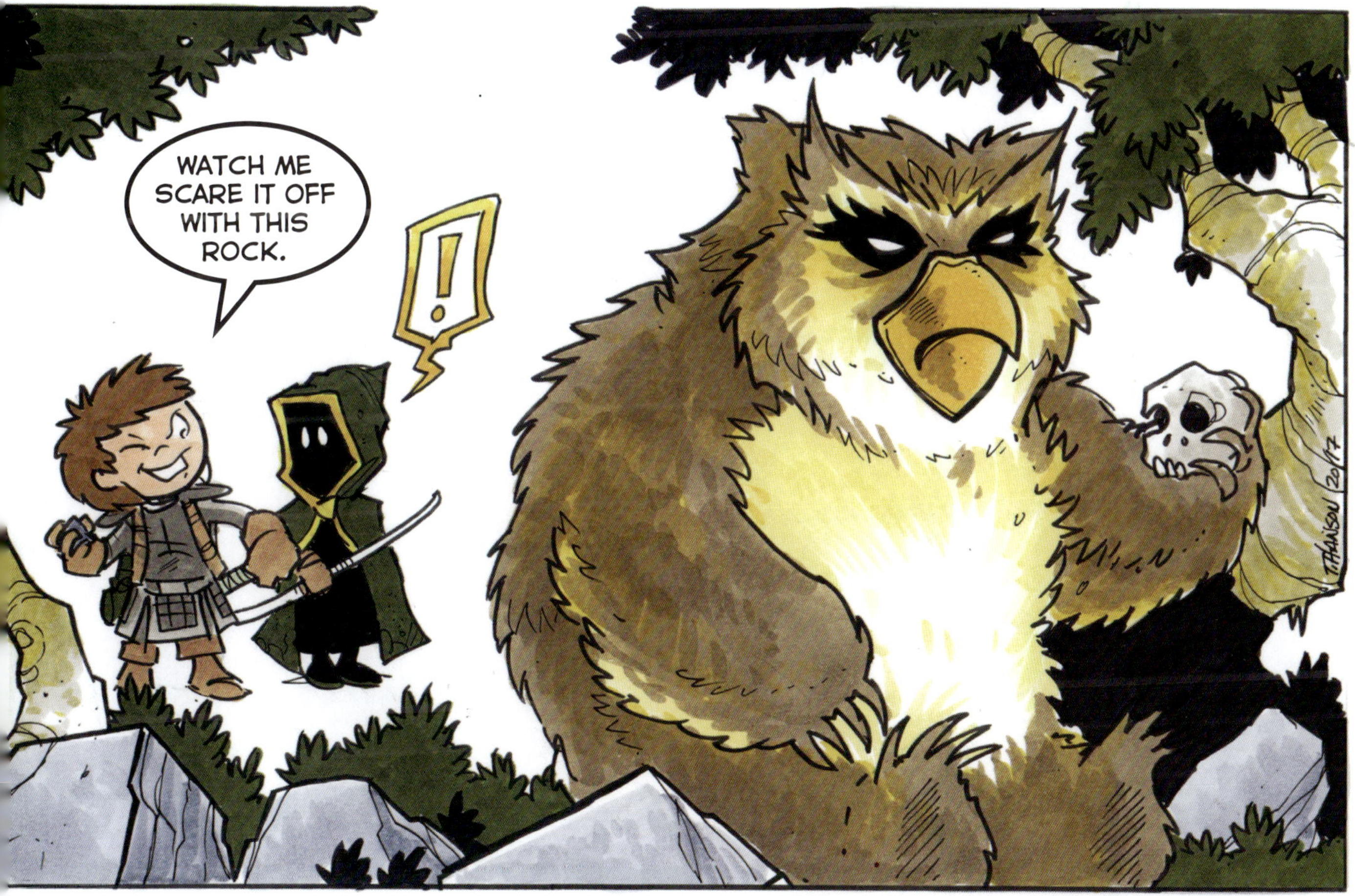

Life of the Party: Realities of an RPG'er

by Travis Hanson

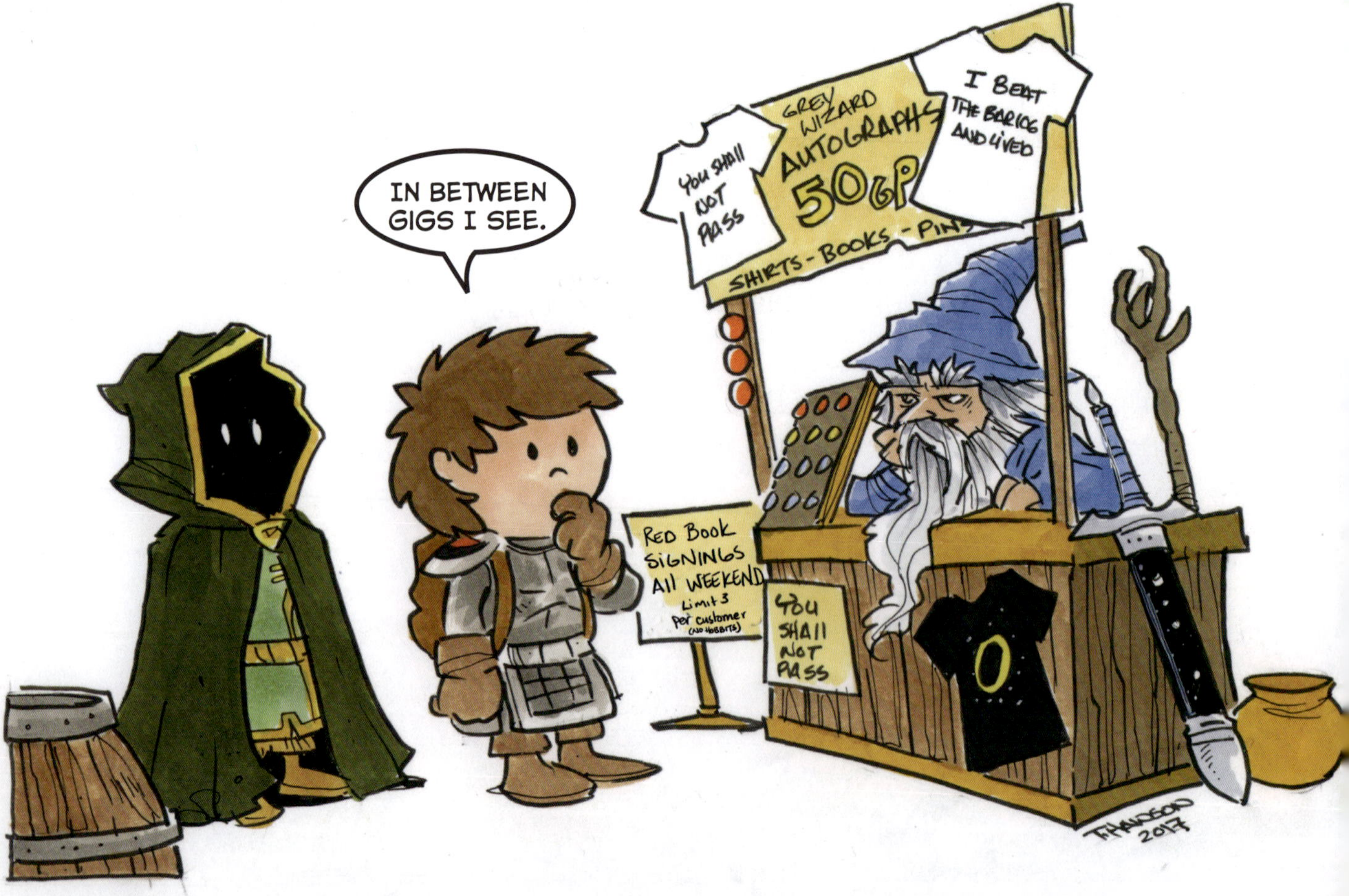

Life of the Party: Realities of an RPG'er

by Travis Hanson

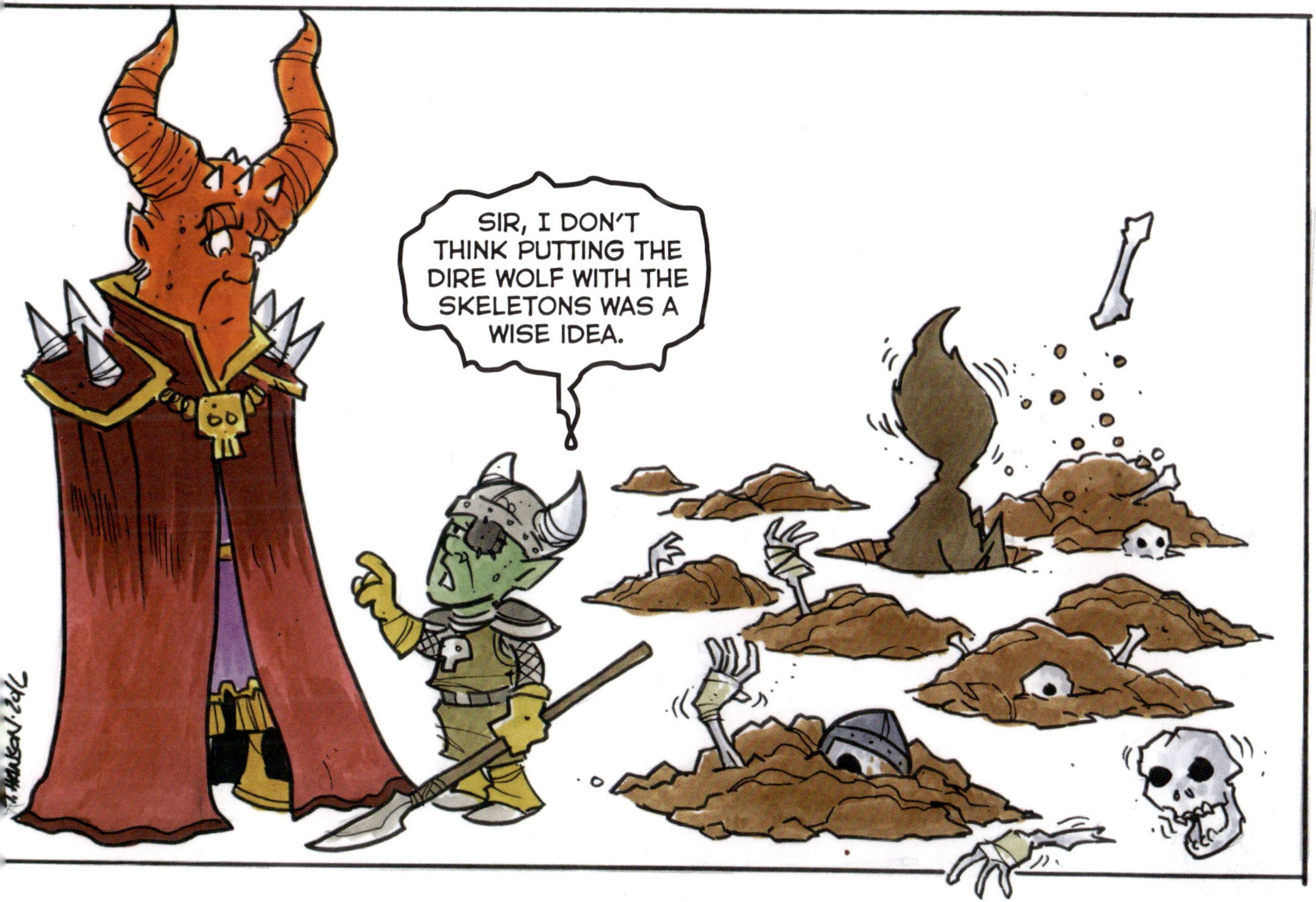

Life of the Party: Realities of an RPG'er by Travis Hanson

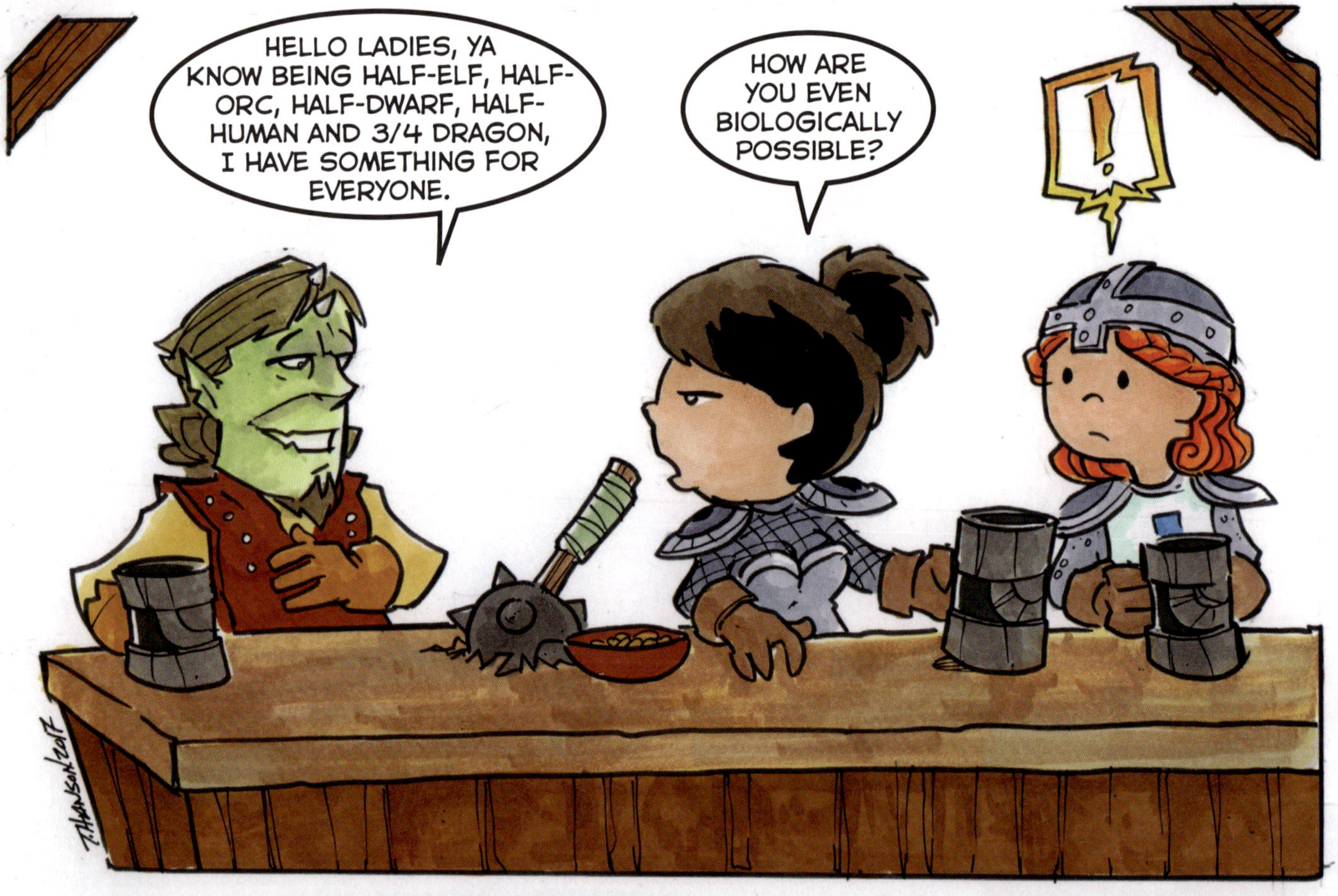

Life of the Party: Realities of an RPG'er by Travis Hanson

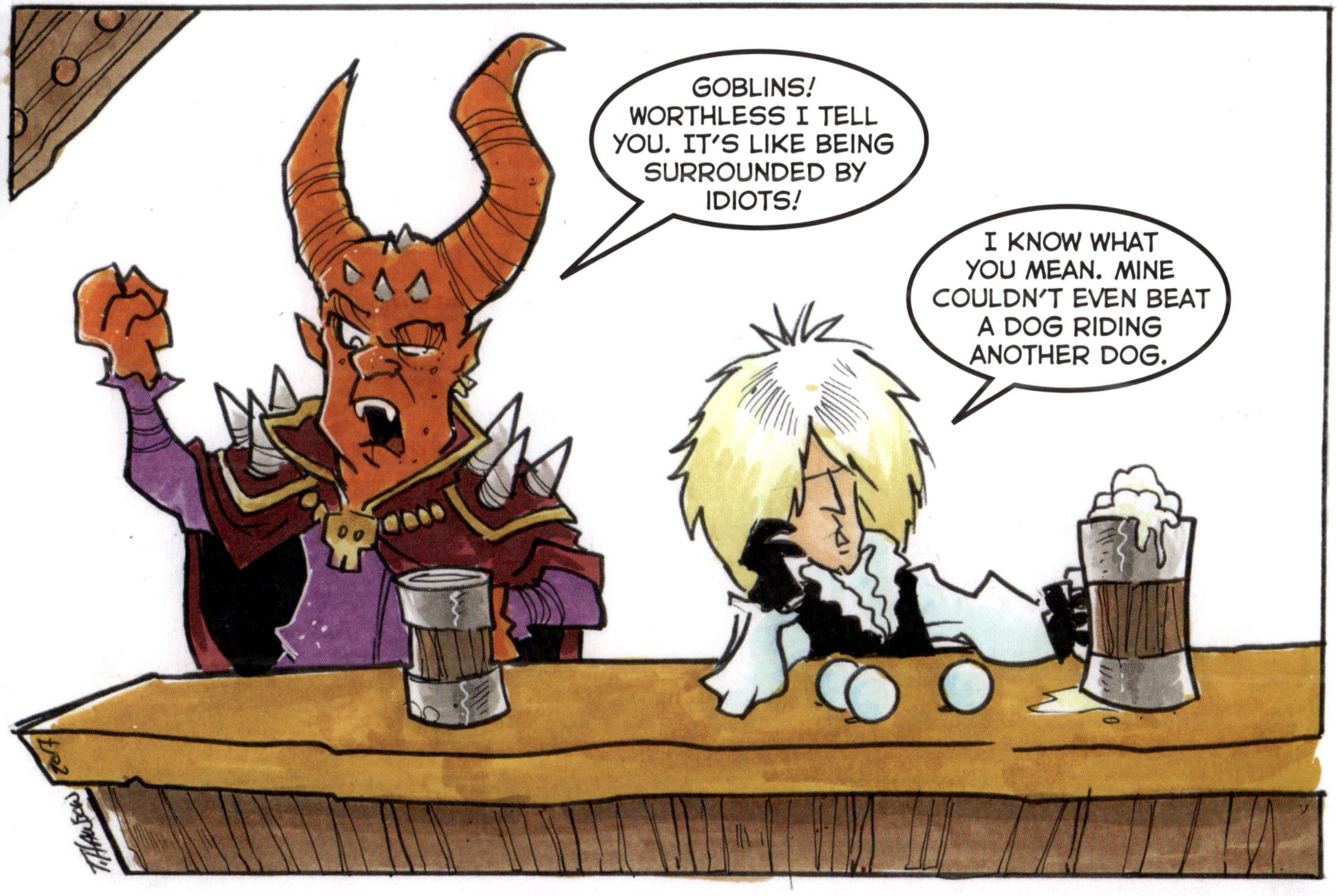

Life of the Party: Realities of an RPG'er

by Travis Hanson

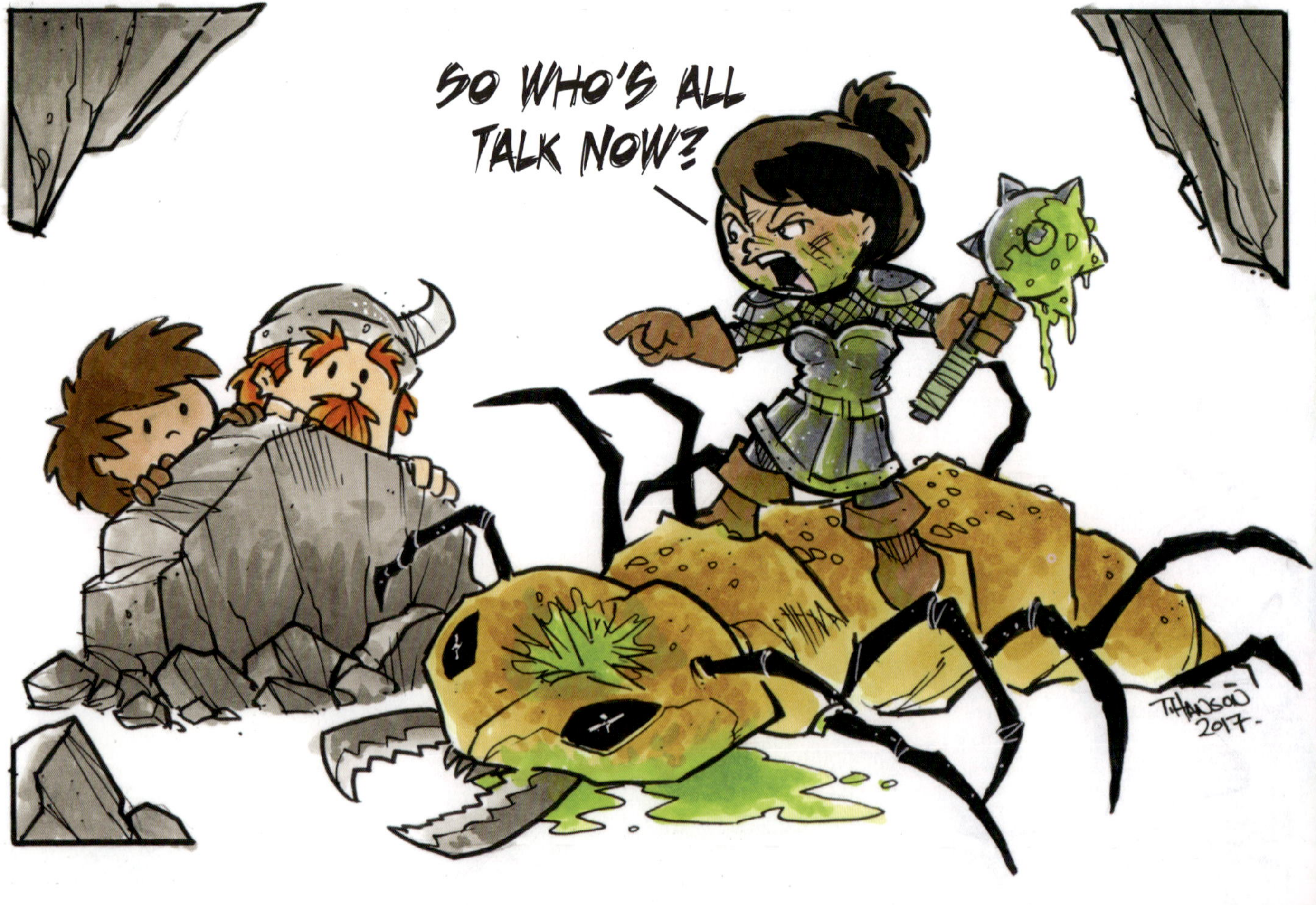

Life of the Party: Realities of an RPG'er

by Travis Hanson

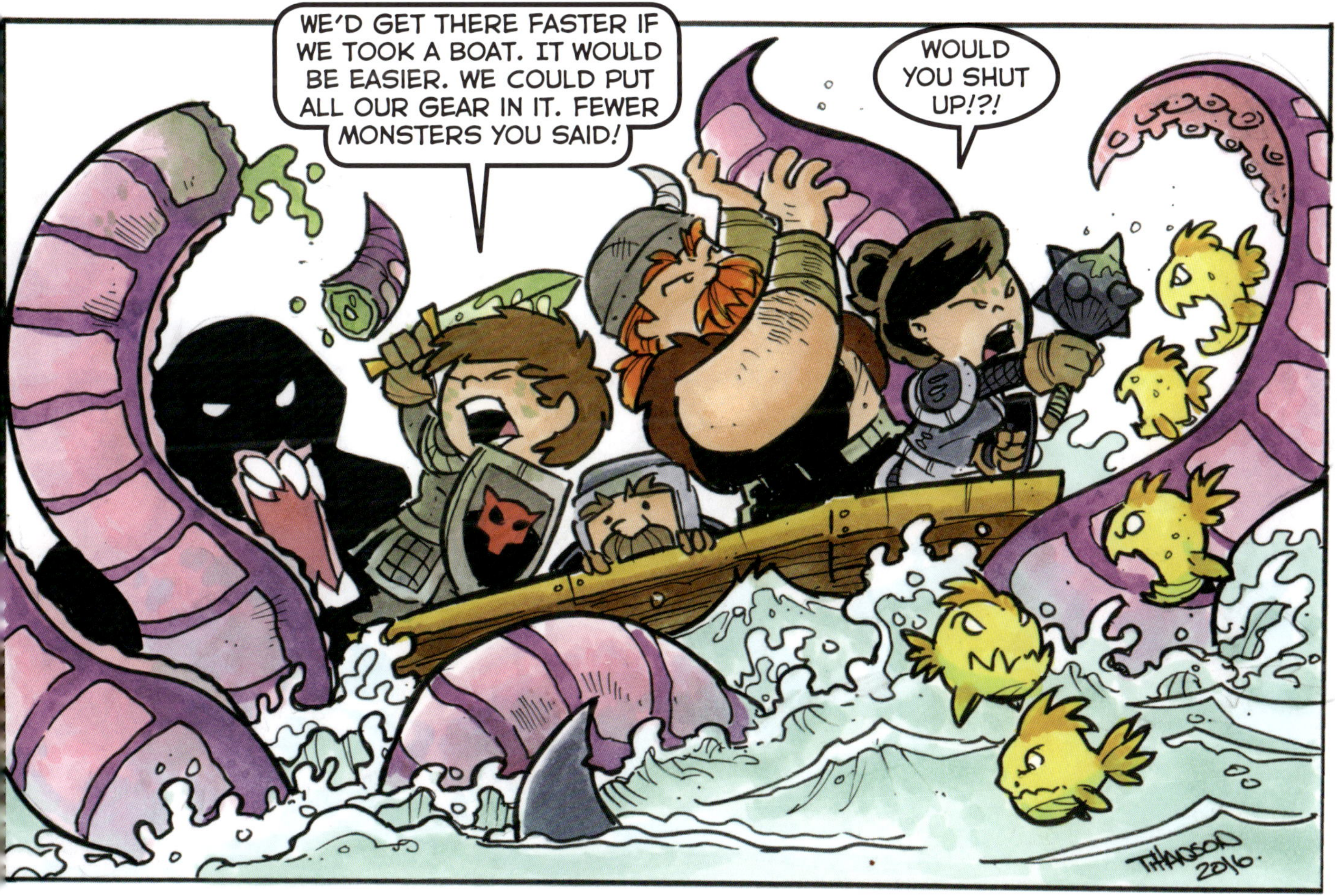

Life of the Party: Realities of an RPG'er

by Travis Hanson

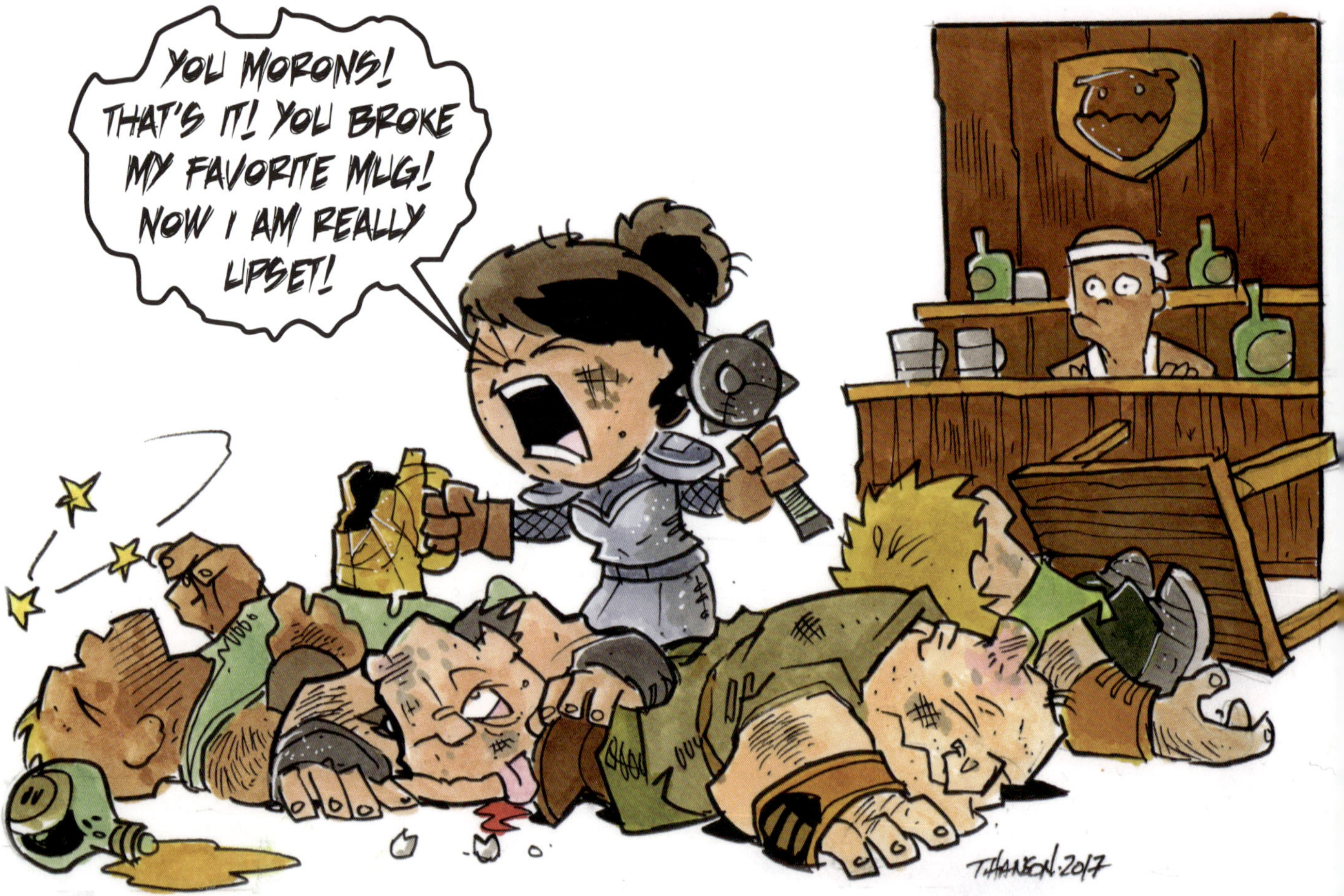

Life of the Party: Realities of an RPG'er

by Travis Hanson

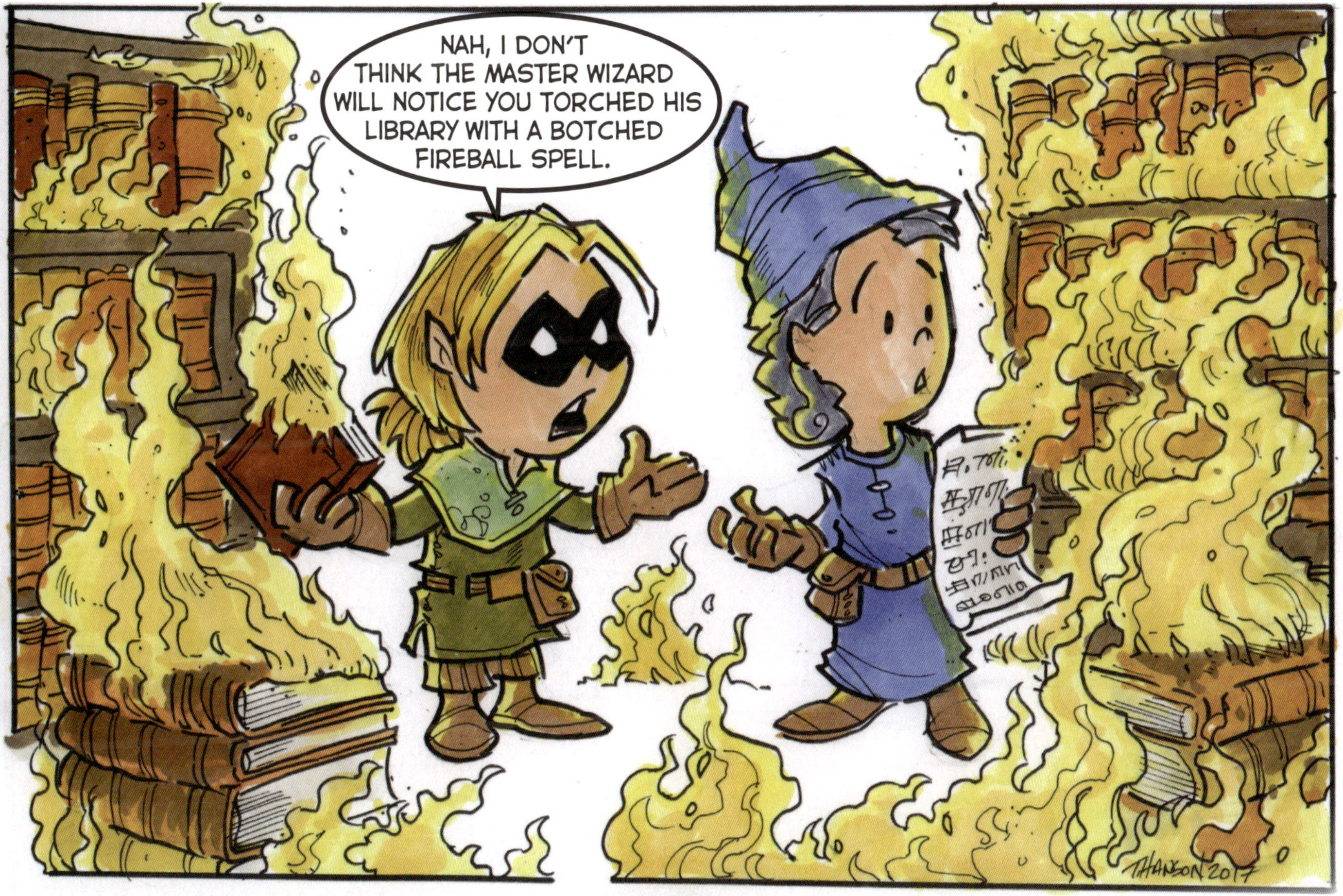

Life of the Party: Realities of an RPG'er — by Travis Hanson

"DON'T WORRY. I SPEAK THEIR LANGUAGE."

Life of the Party: Realities of an RPG'er

by Travis Hanson

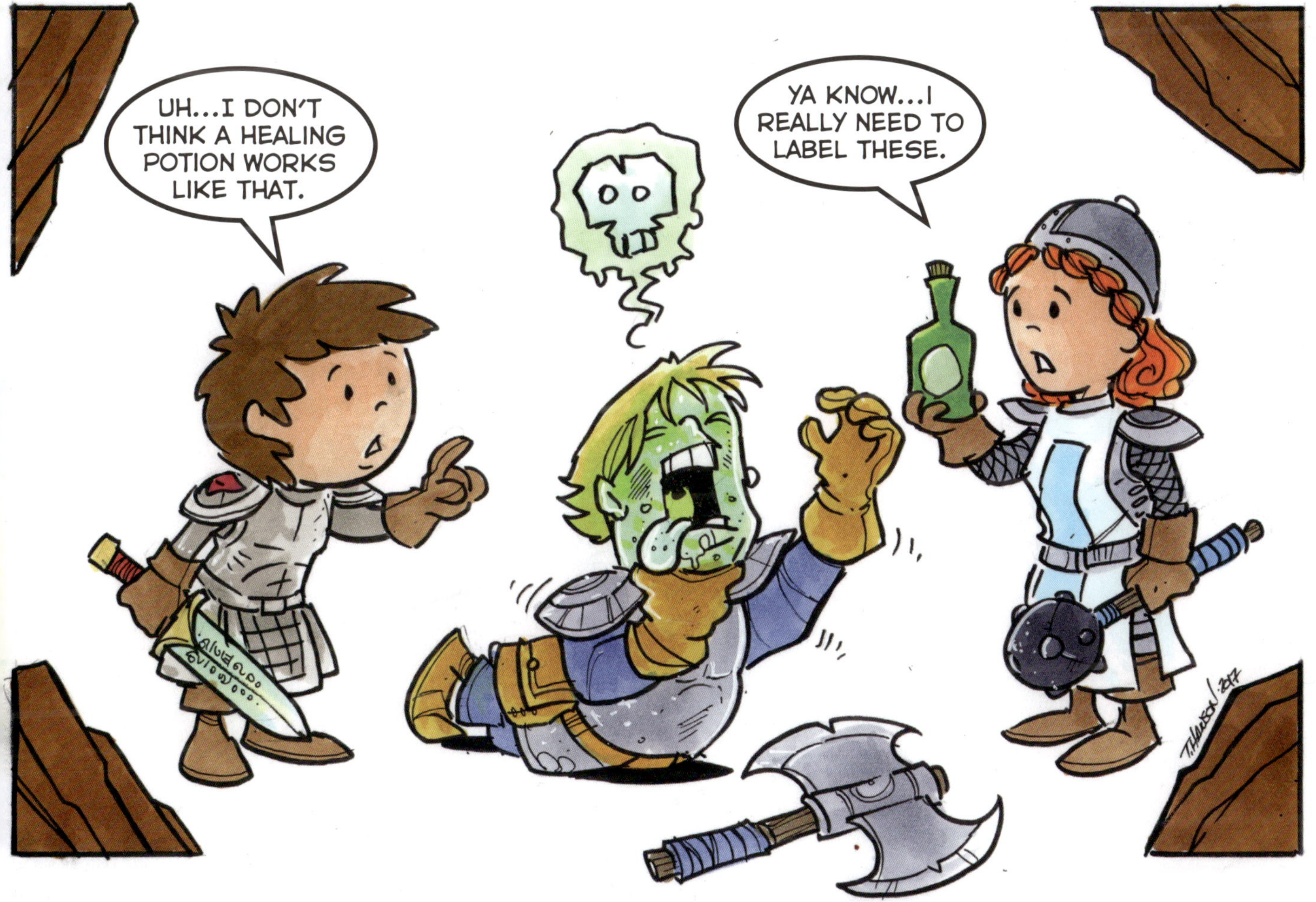

Life of the Party: Realities of an RPG'er

by Travis Hanson

"WHY CAN'T YOU LOOK THAT GOOD IN ARMOR?"

Life of the Party: Realities of an RPG'er by Travis Hanson

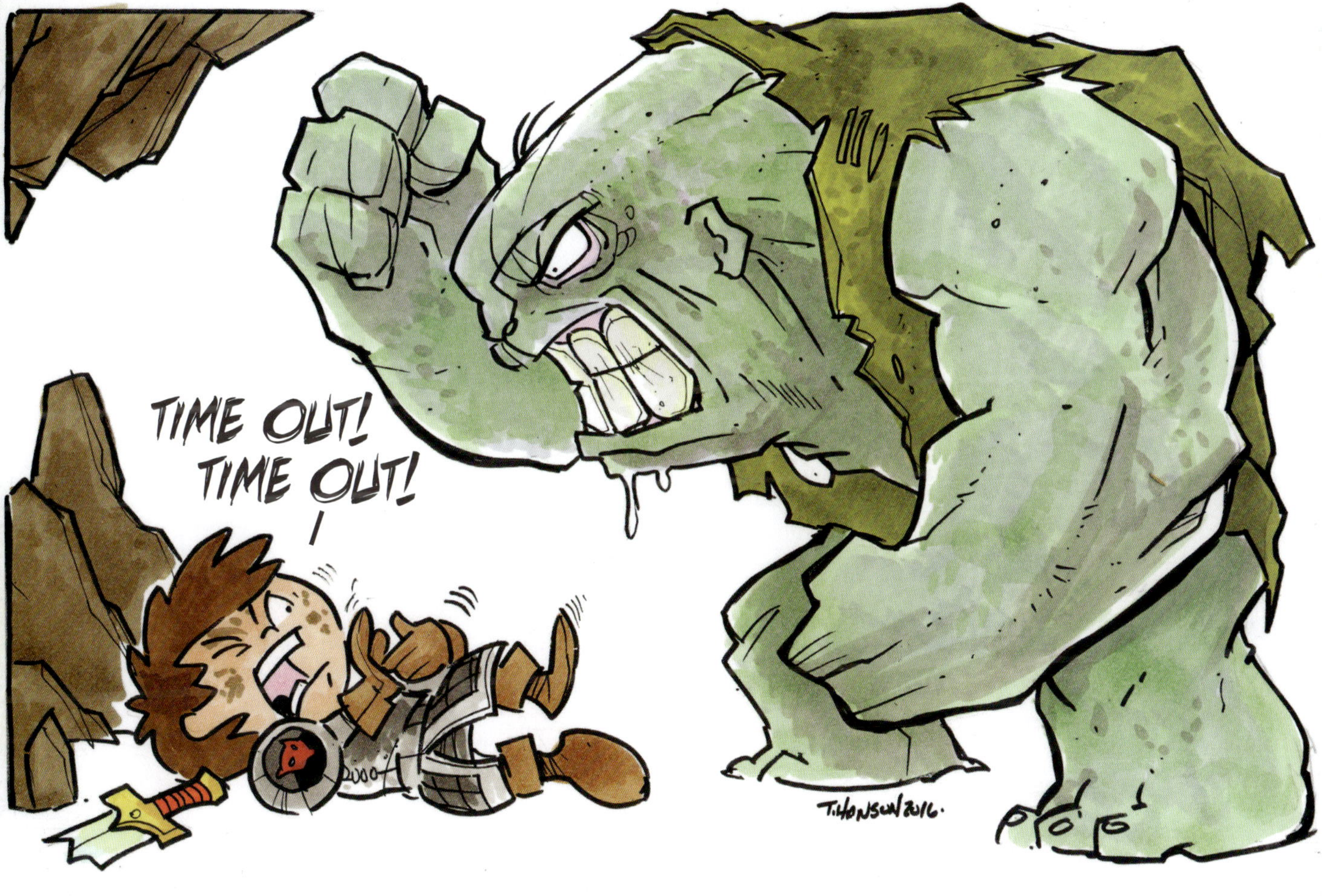

Life of the Party: Realities of an RPG'er

by Travis Hanson

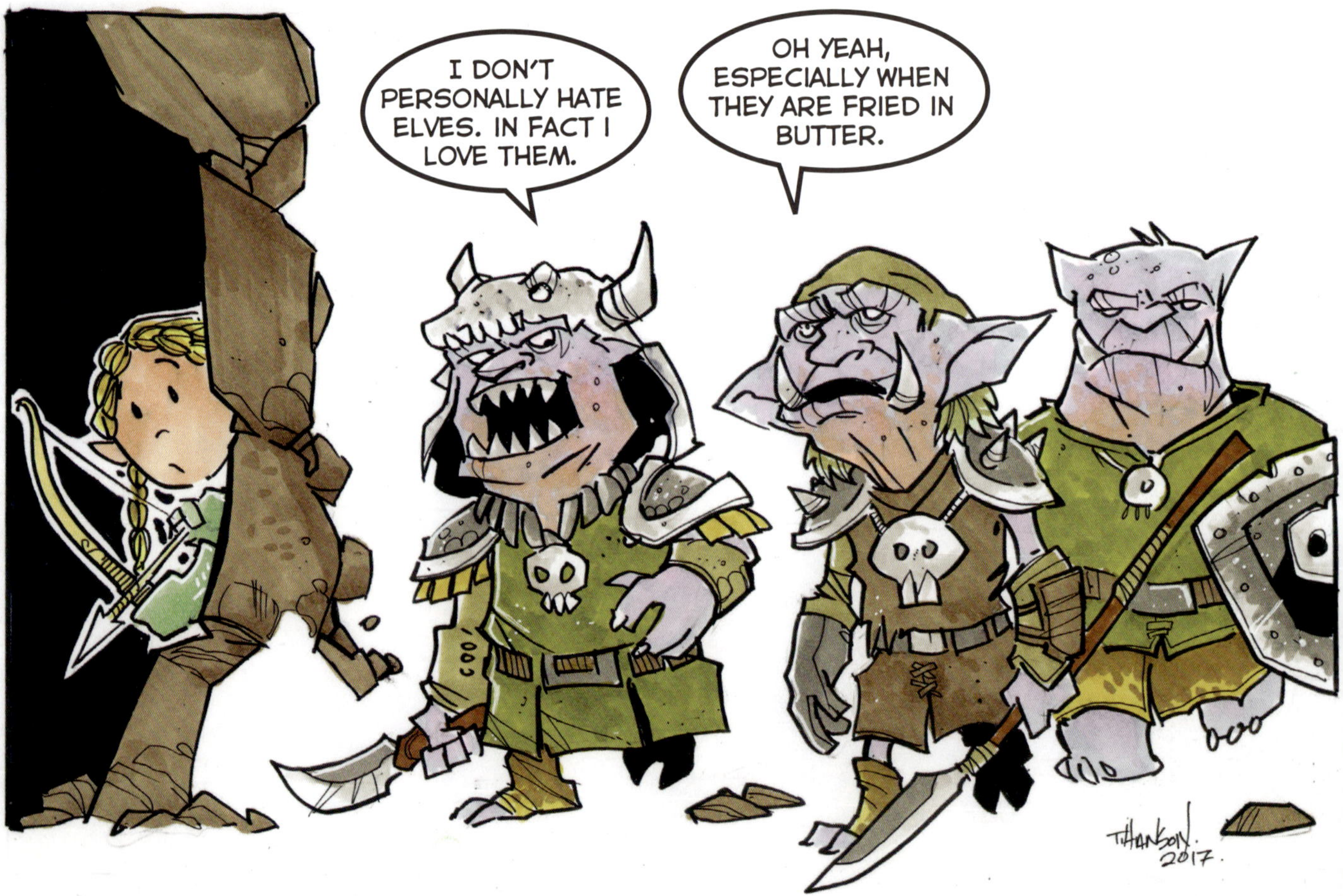

Life of the Party: Realities of an RPG'er — by Travis Hanson

Life of the Party: Realities of an RPG'er

by Travis Hanson

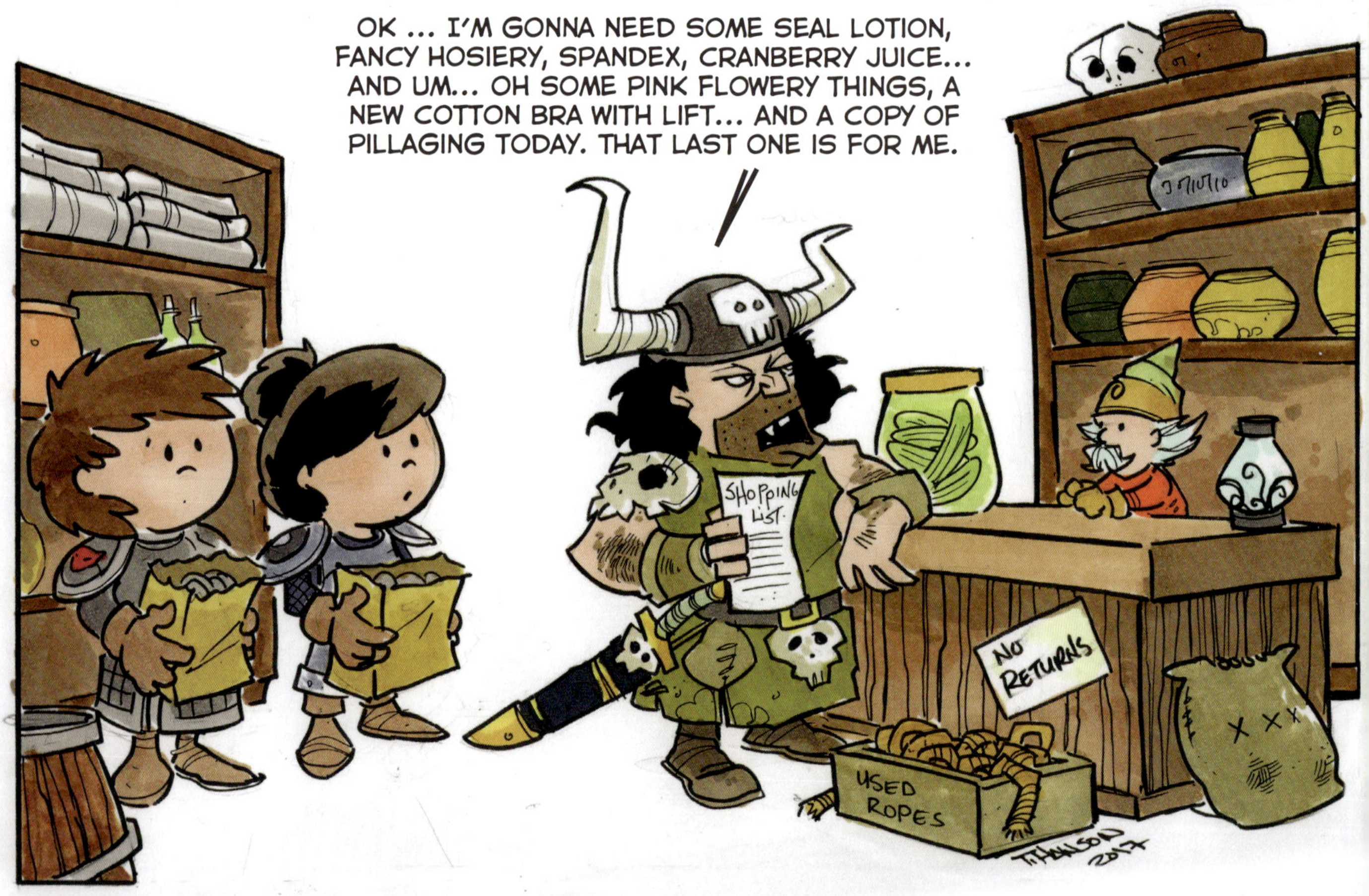

Life of the Party: Realities of an RPG'er

by Travis Hanson

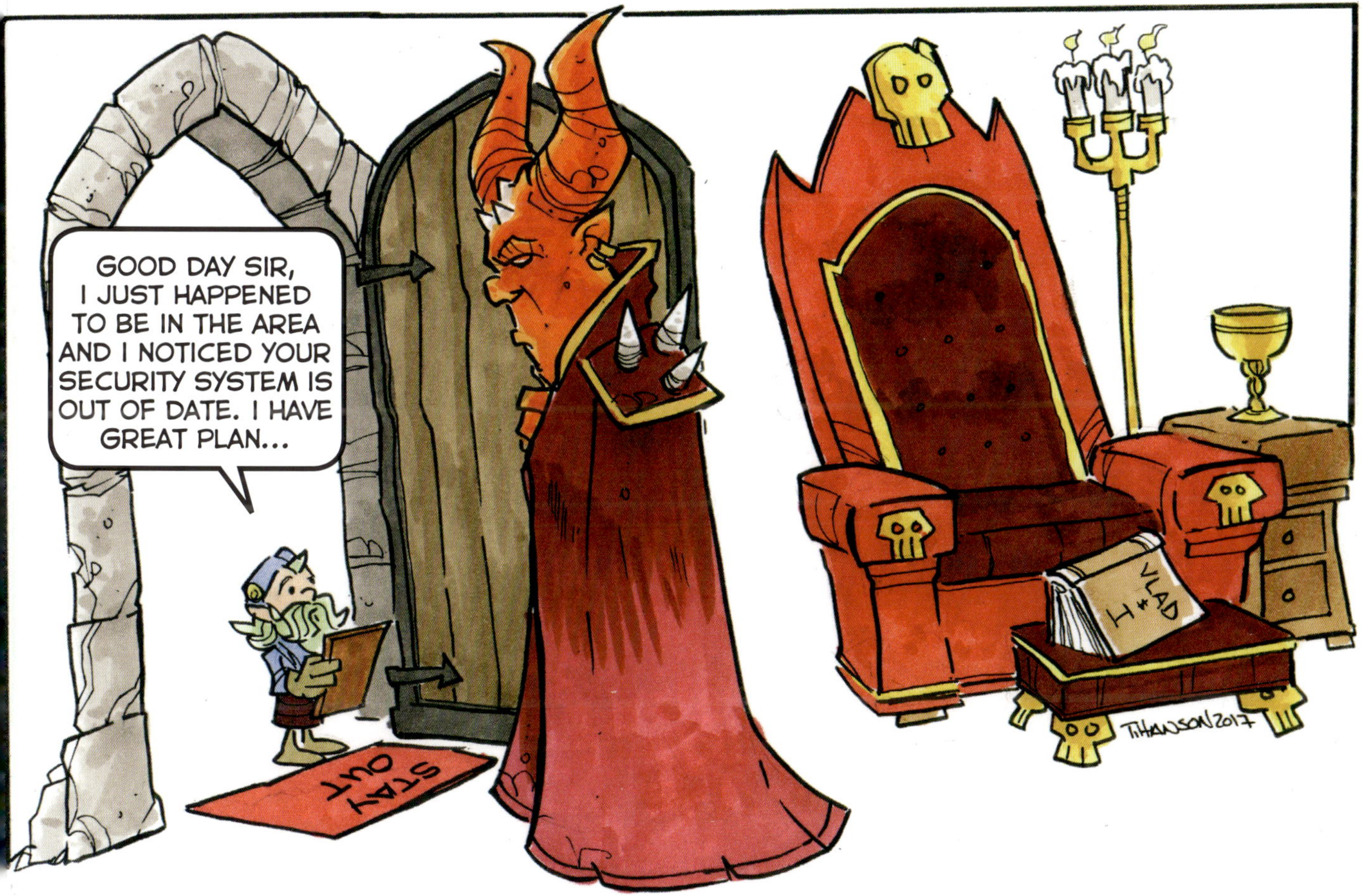

Life of the Party: Realities of an RPG'er

by Travis Hanson

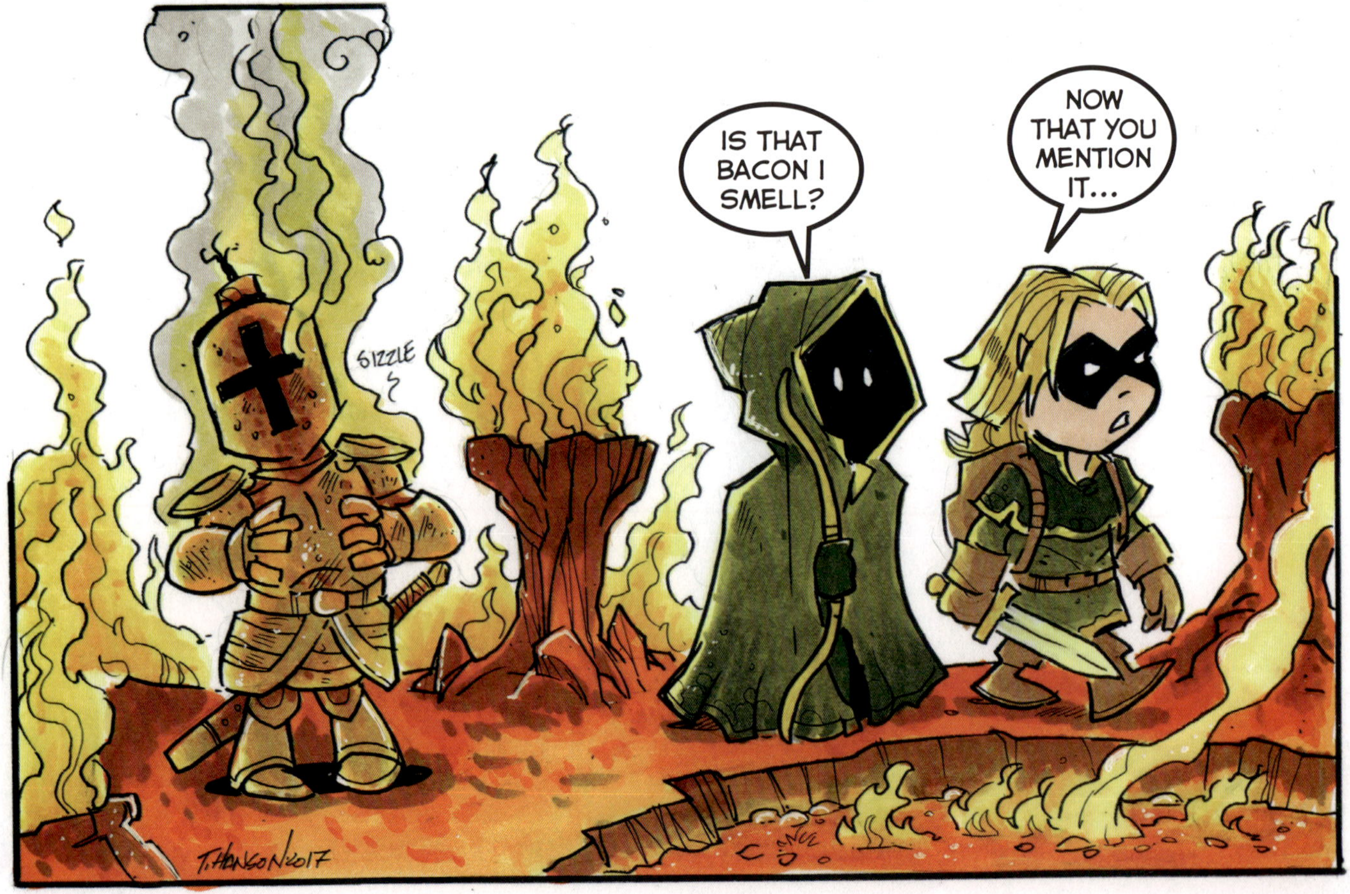

Life of the Party: Realities of an RPG'er

by Travis Hanson

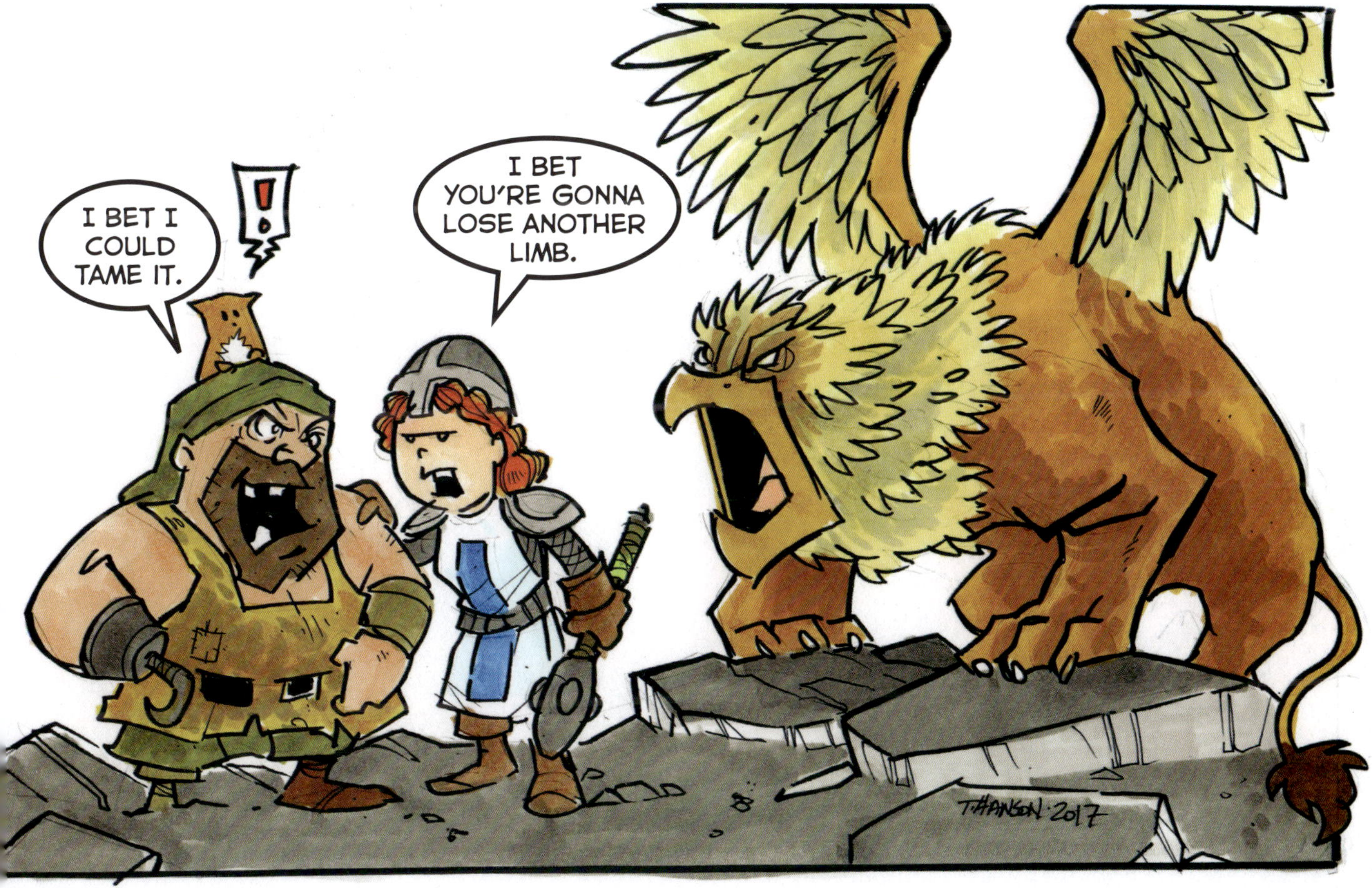

Life of the Party: Realities of an RPG'er

by Travis Hanson

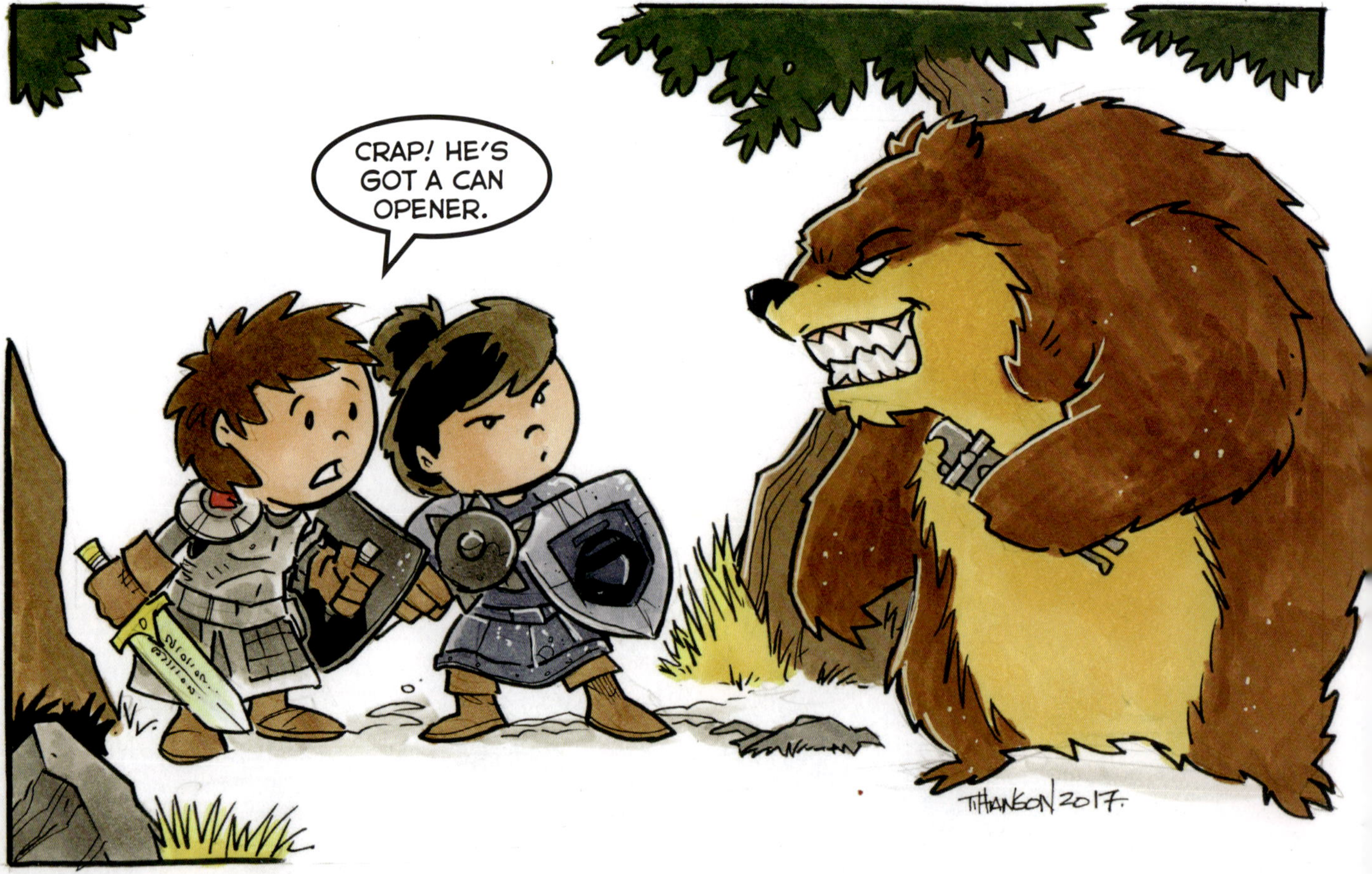

Life of the Party: Realities of an RPG'er

by Travis Hanson

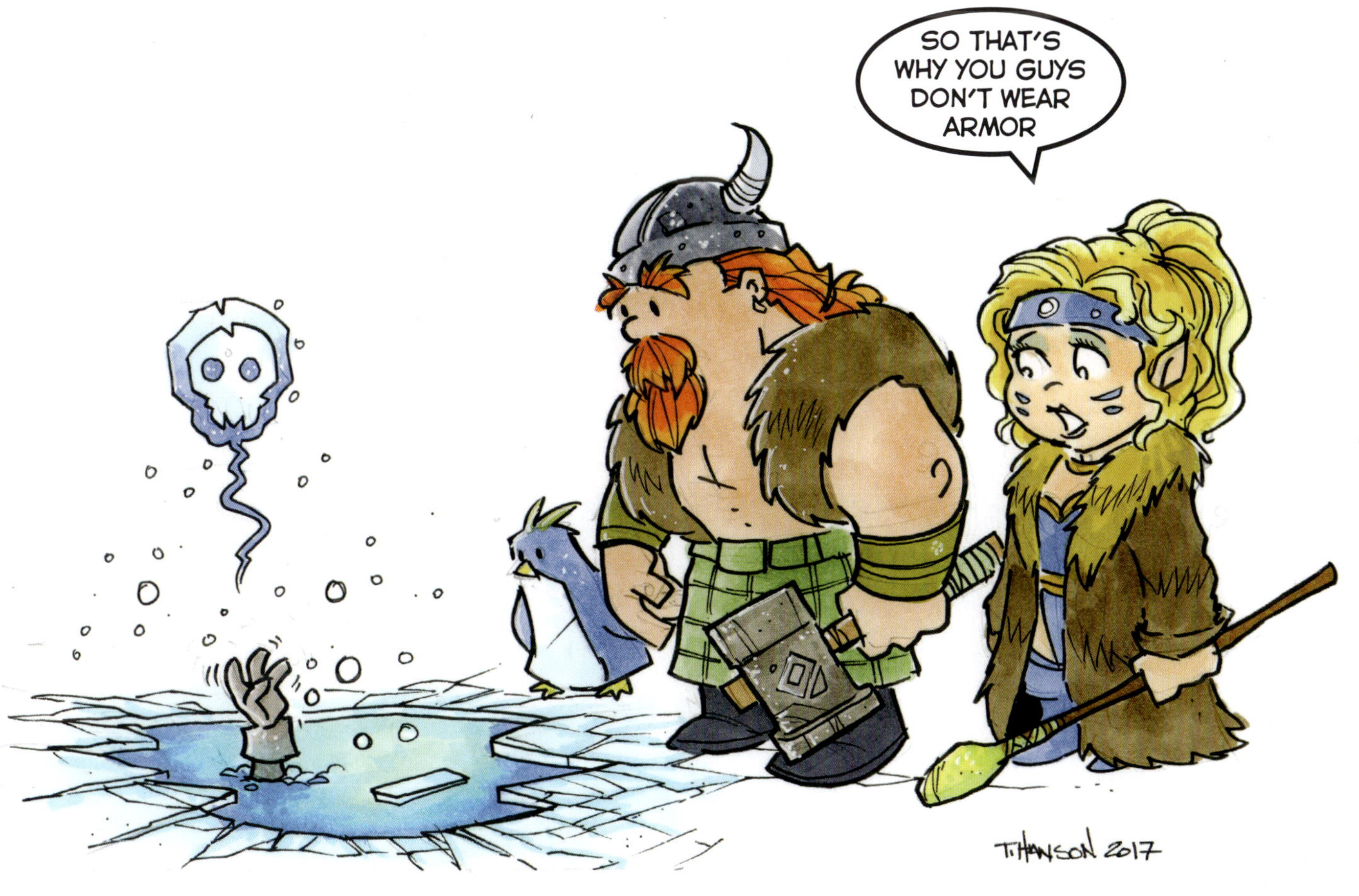

Life of the Party: Realities of an RPG'er
by Travis Hanson

OK, ONE OF US IS GONNA HAVE TO SUCK THE POISON OUT. I SAY WE FLIP FOR IT.

YOU'RE ON YOUR OWN.

ACK!

Life of the Party: Realities of an RPG'er

by Travis Hanson

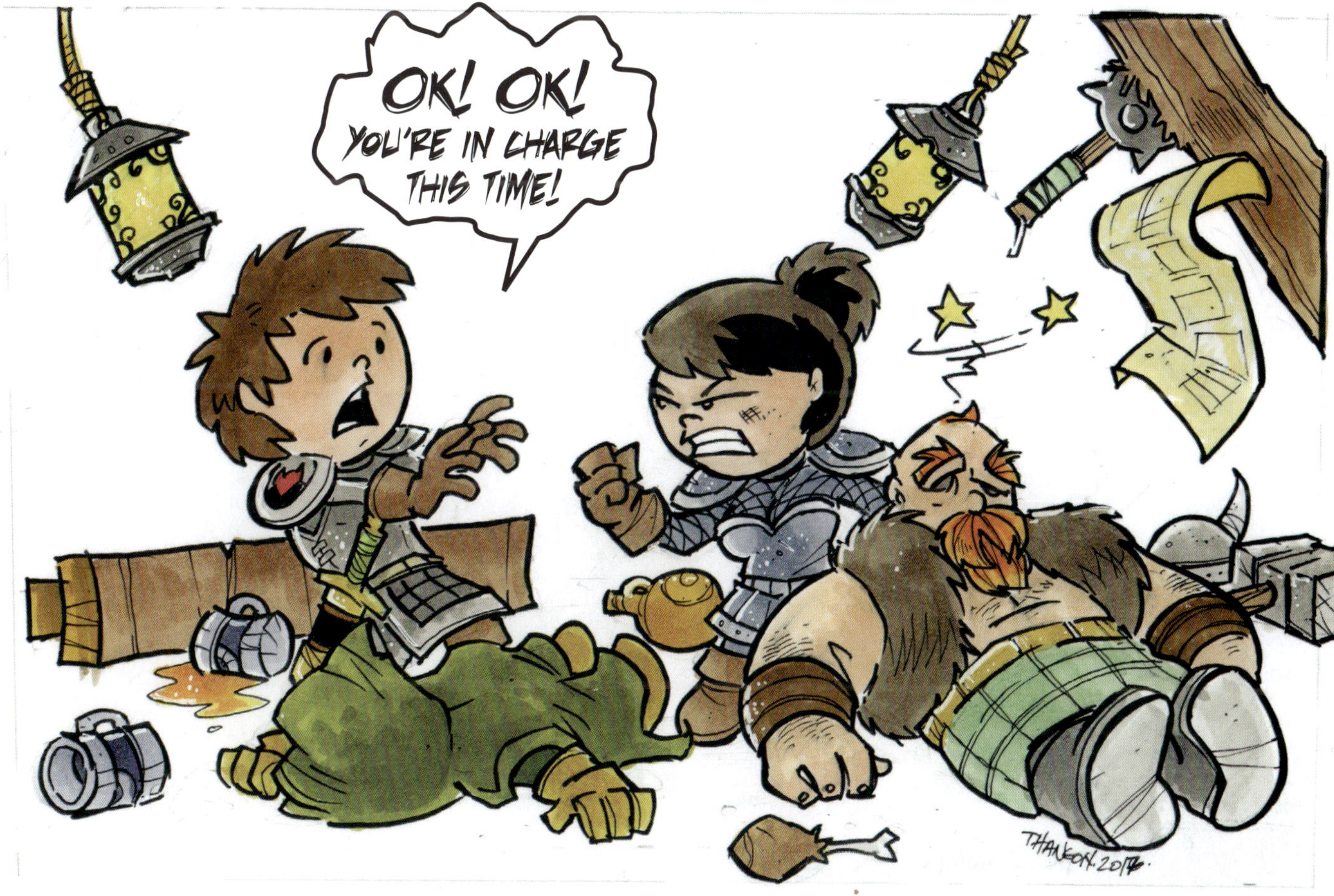

Life of the Party: Realities of an RPG'er

by Travis Hanson

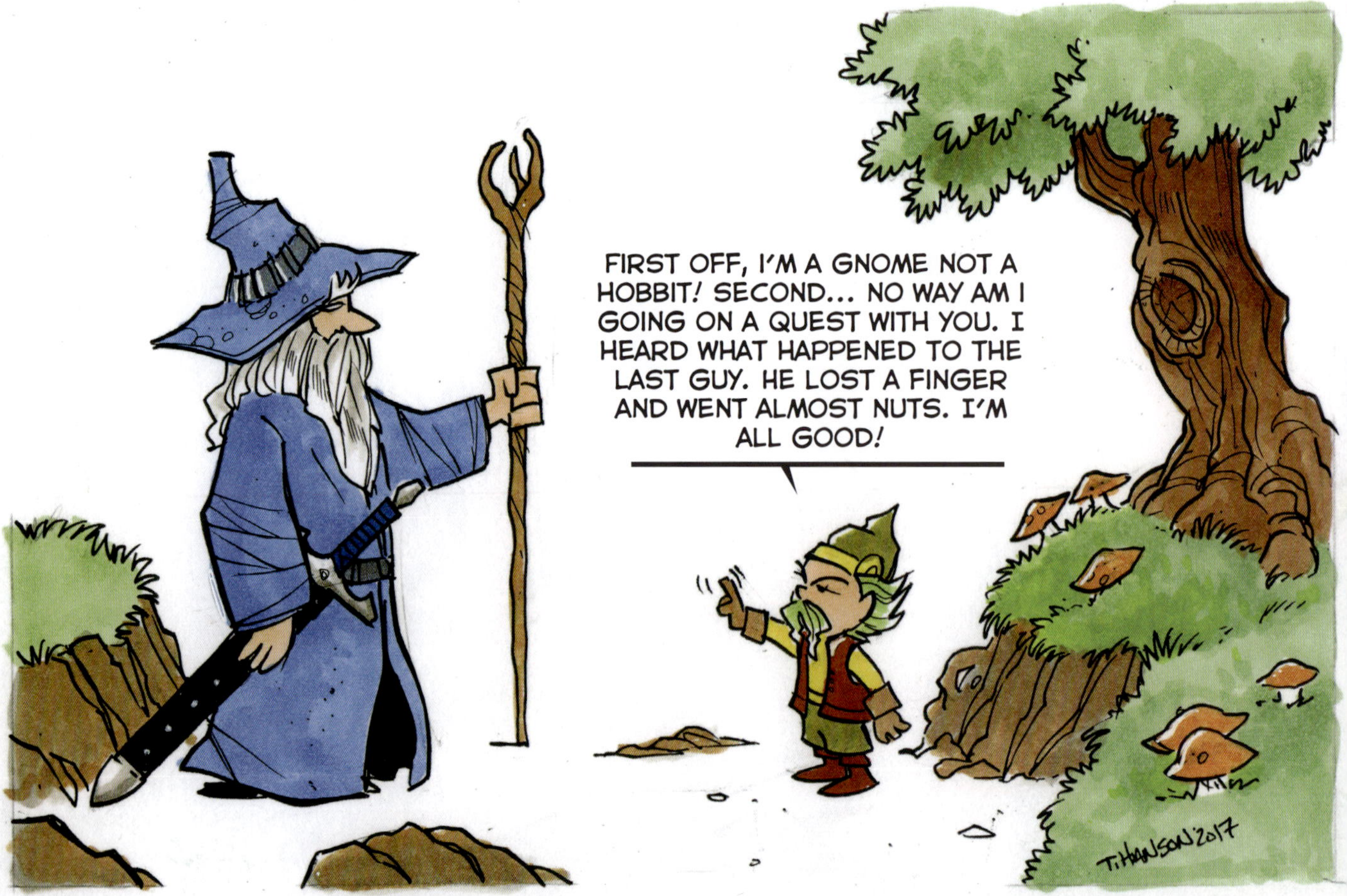

Life of the Party: Realities of an RPG'er

by Travis Hanson

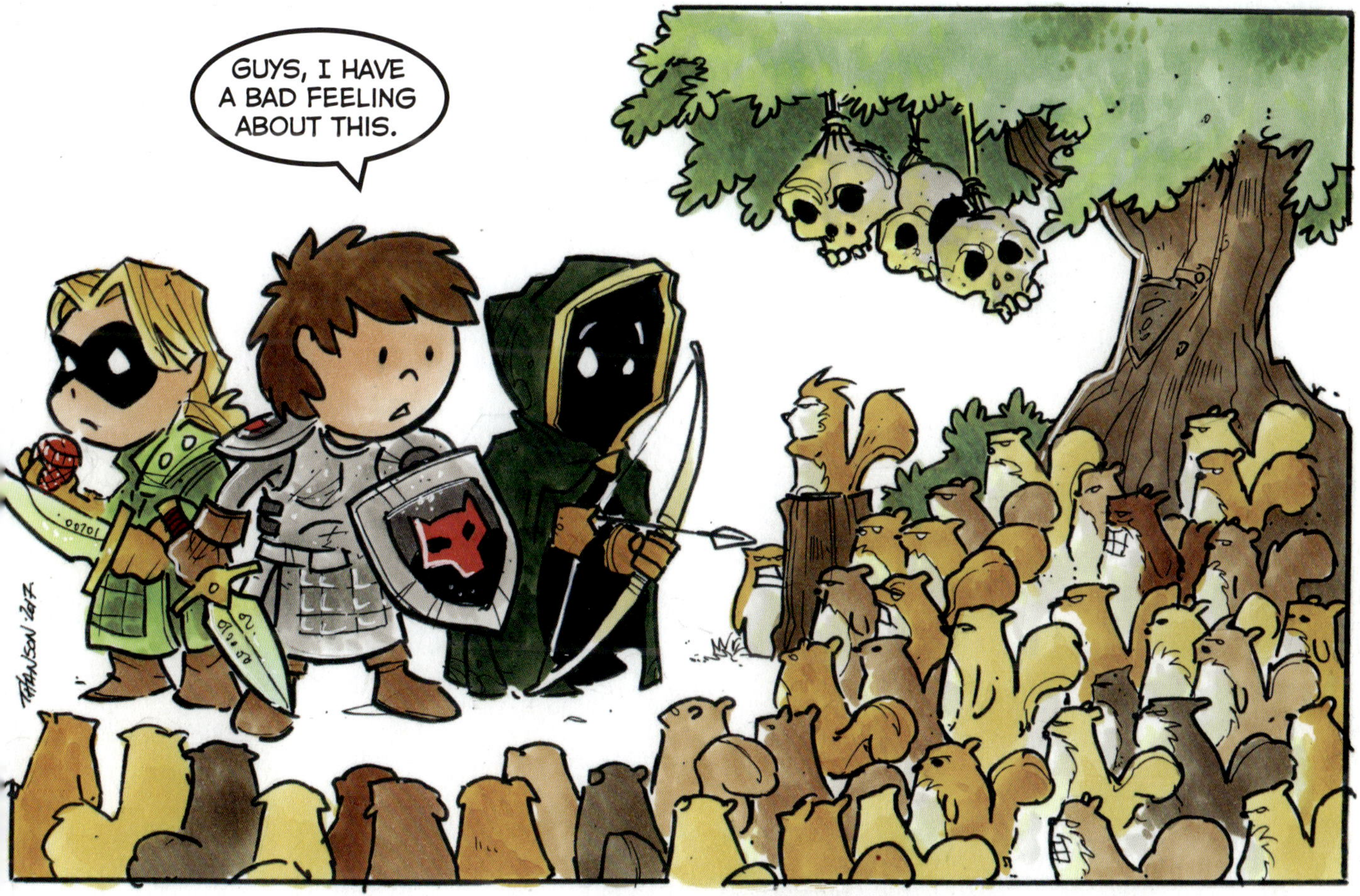

Life of the Party: Realities of an RPG'er by Travis Hanson

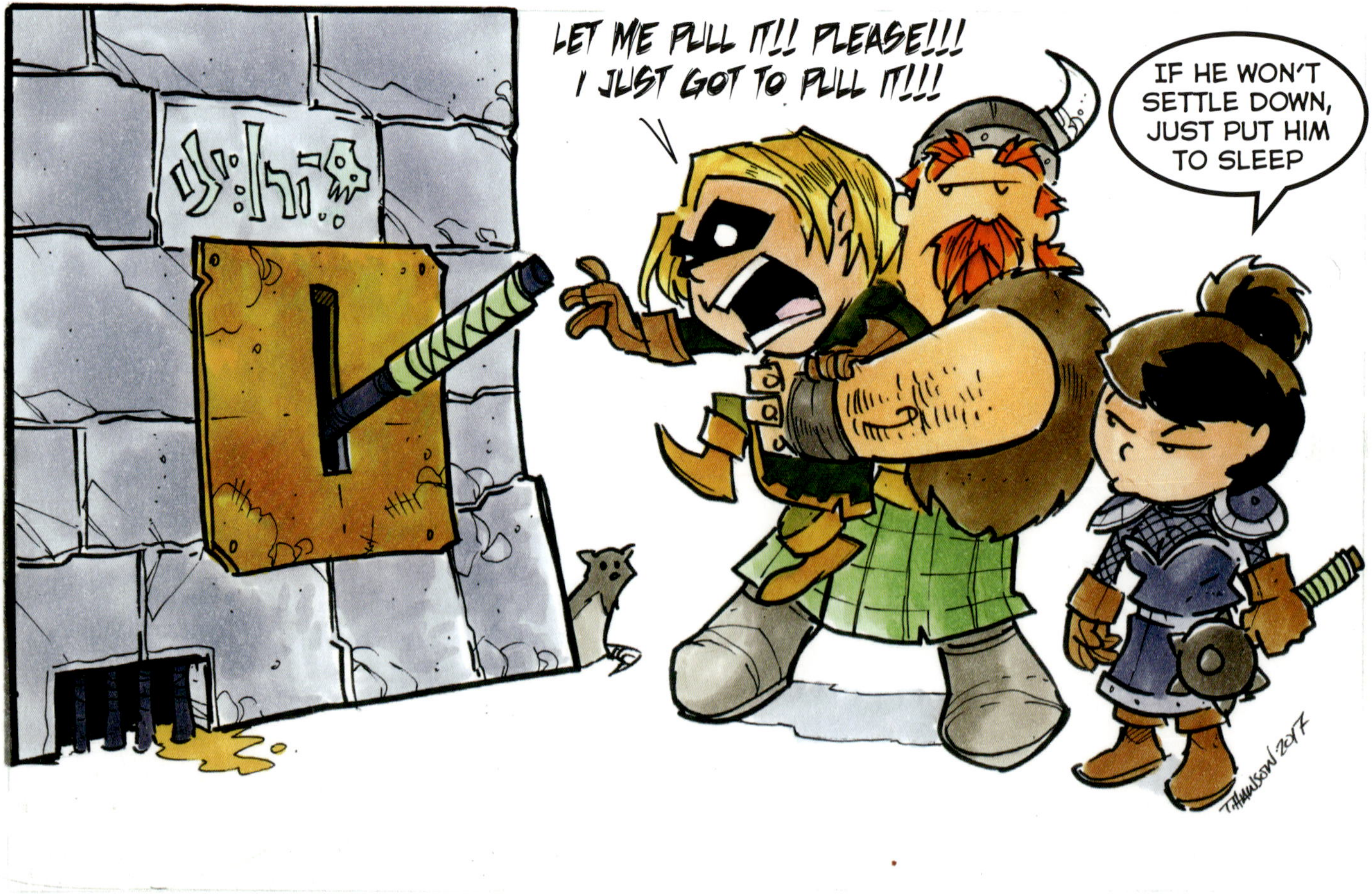

Life of the Party: Realities of an RPG'er

by Travis Hanson

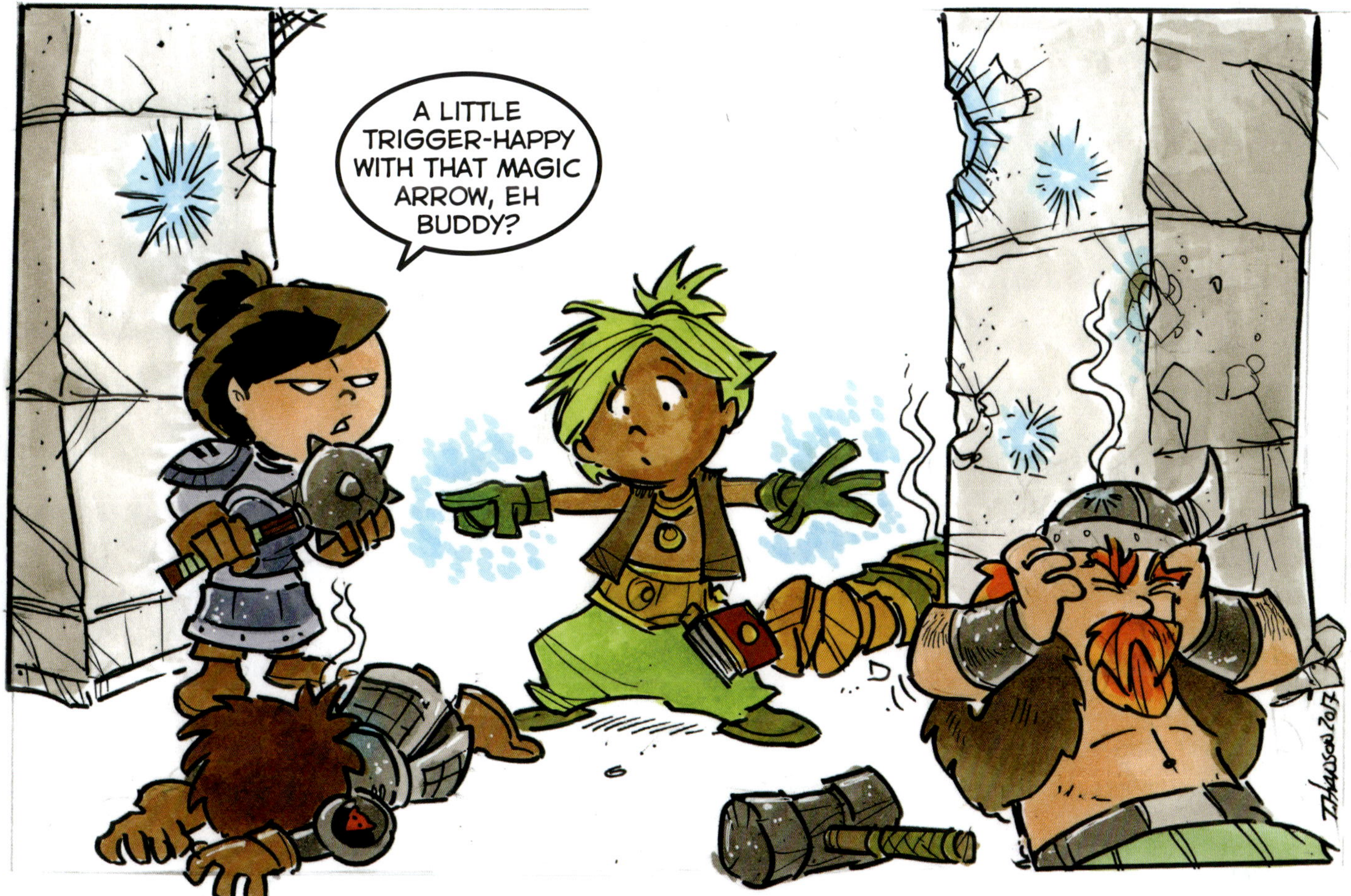

Life of the Party: Realities of an RPG'er

by Travis Hanson

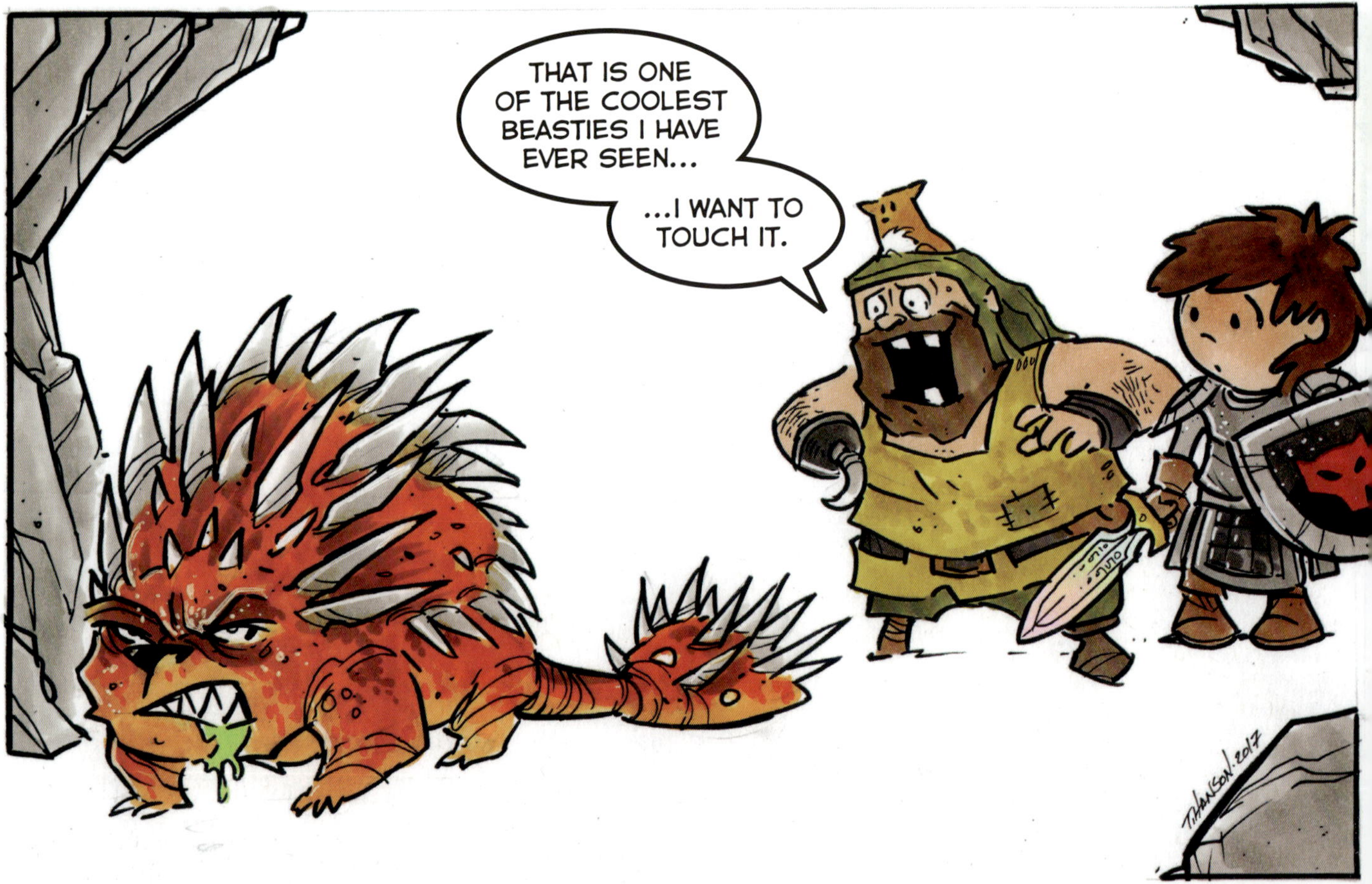

Life of the Party: Realities of an RPG'er

by Travis Hanson

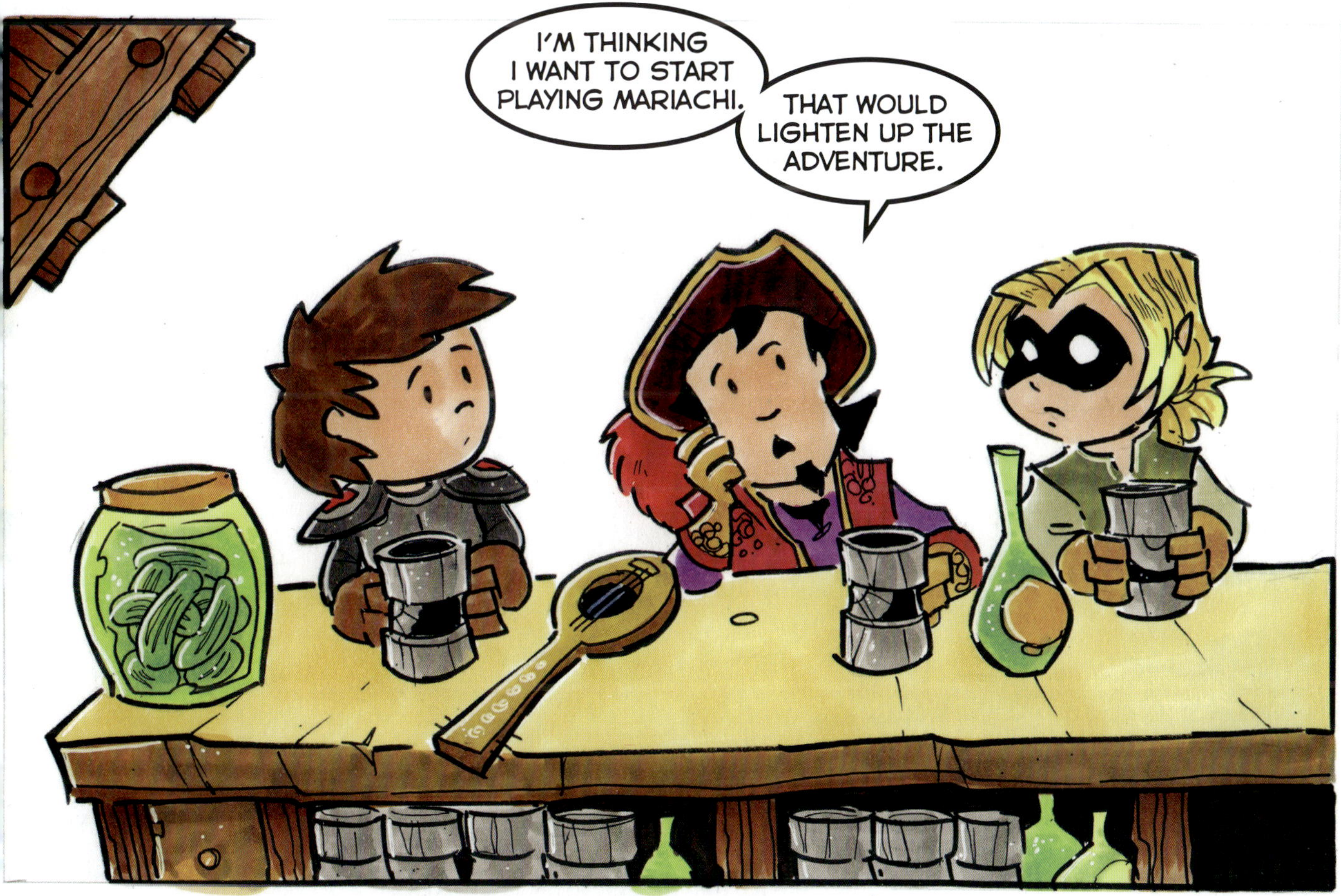

Life of the Party: Realities of an RPG'er

by Travis Hanson

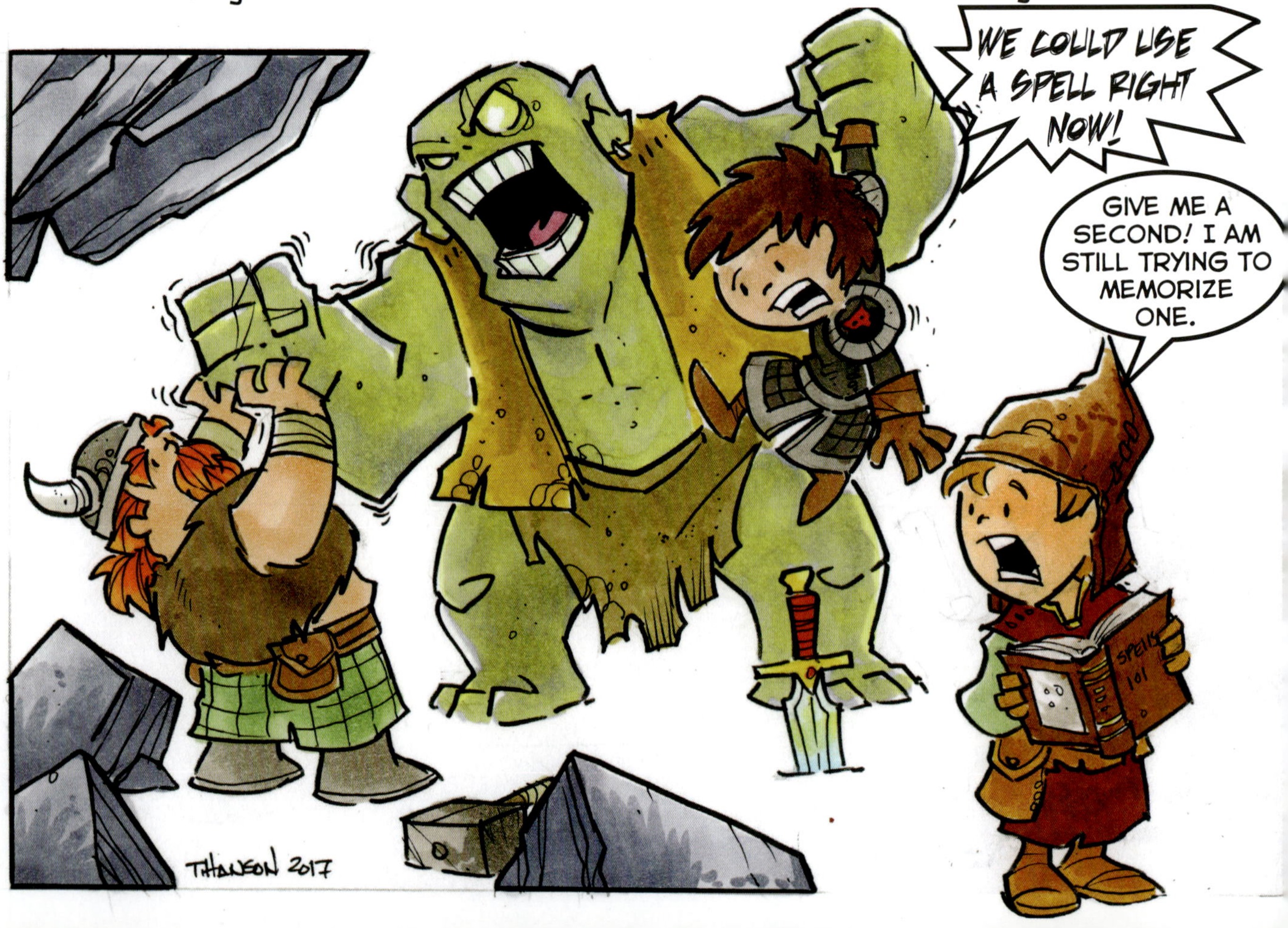

Life of the Party: Realities of an RPG'er by Travis Hanson

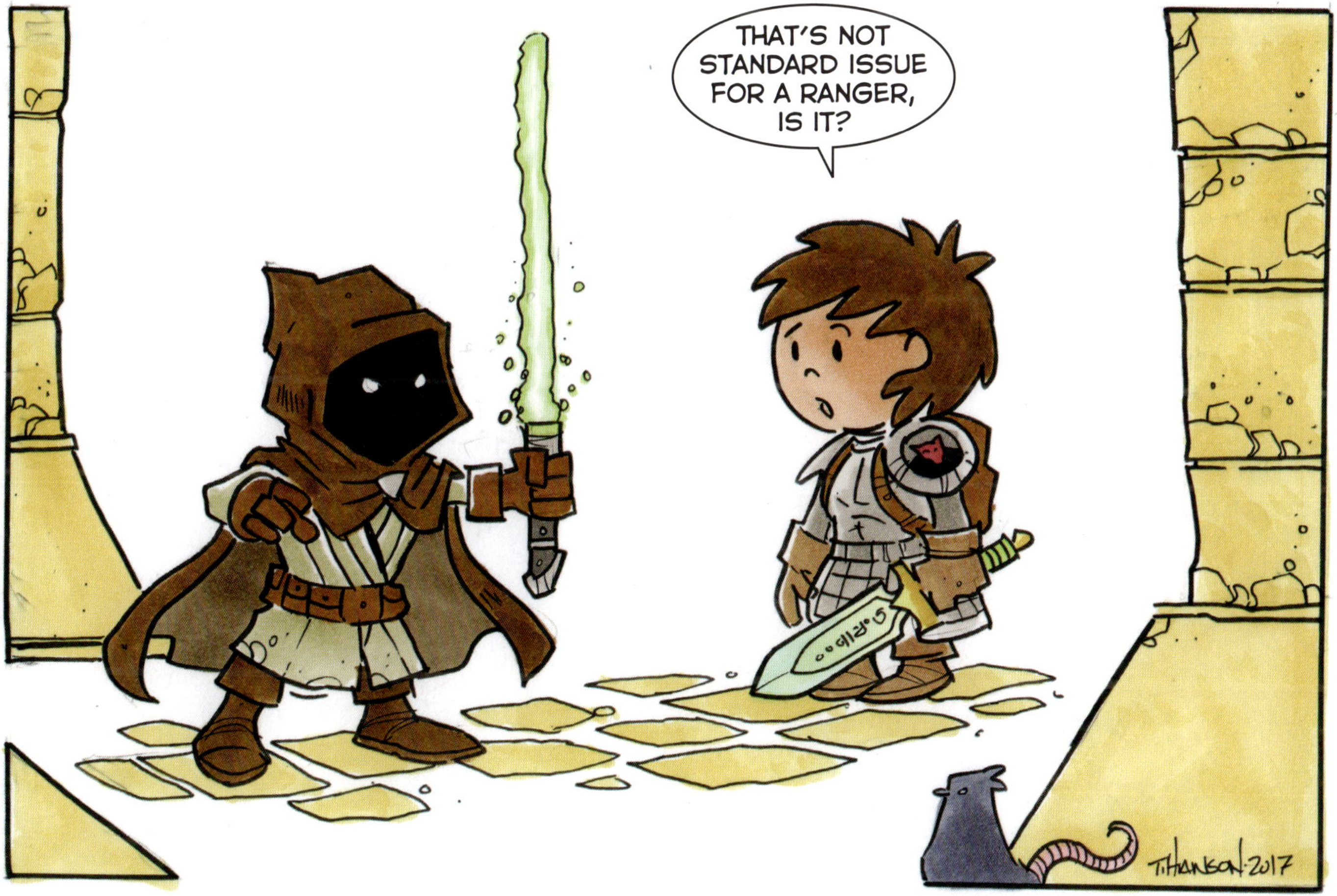

Life of the Party: Realities of an RPG'er

by Travis Hanson

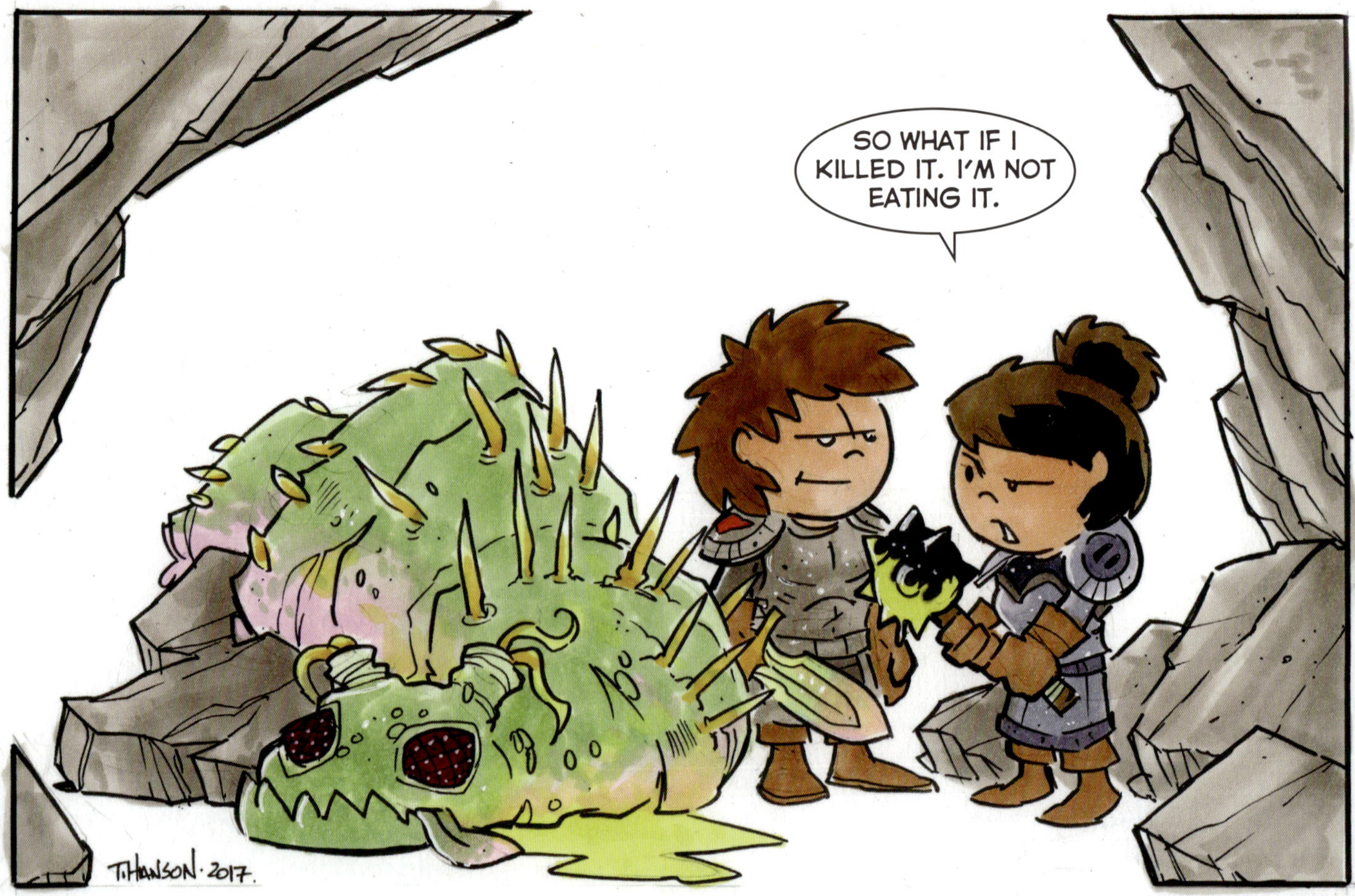

Life of the Party: Realities of an RPG'er

by Travis Hanson

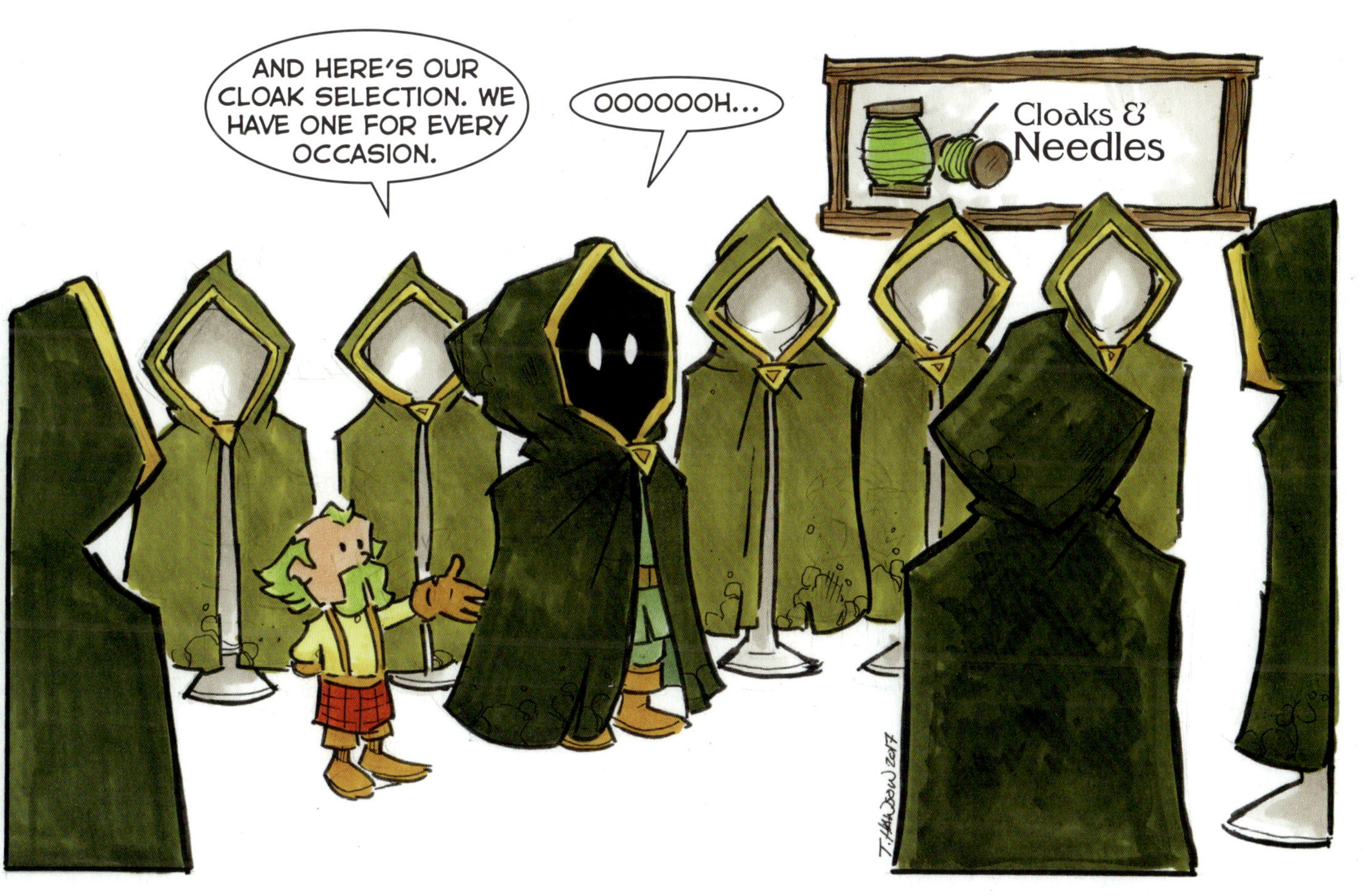

Life of the Party: Realities of an RPG'er

by Travis Hanson

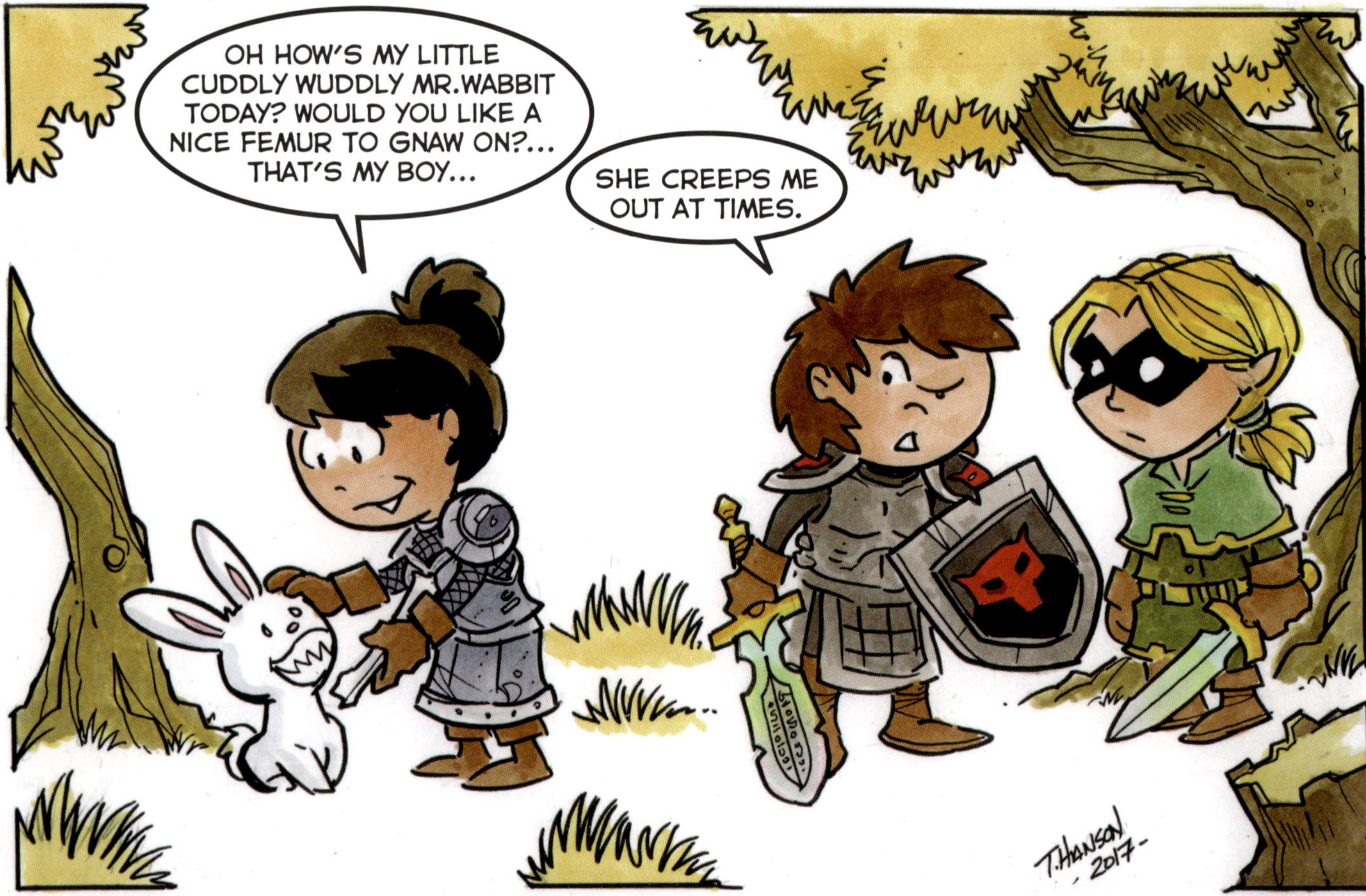

Life of the Party: Realities of an RPG'er

by Travis Hanson

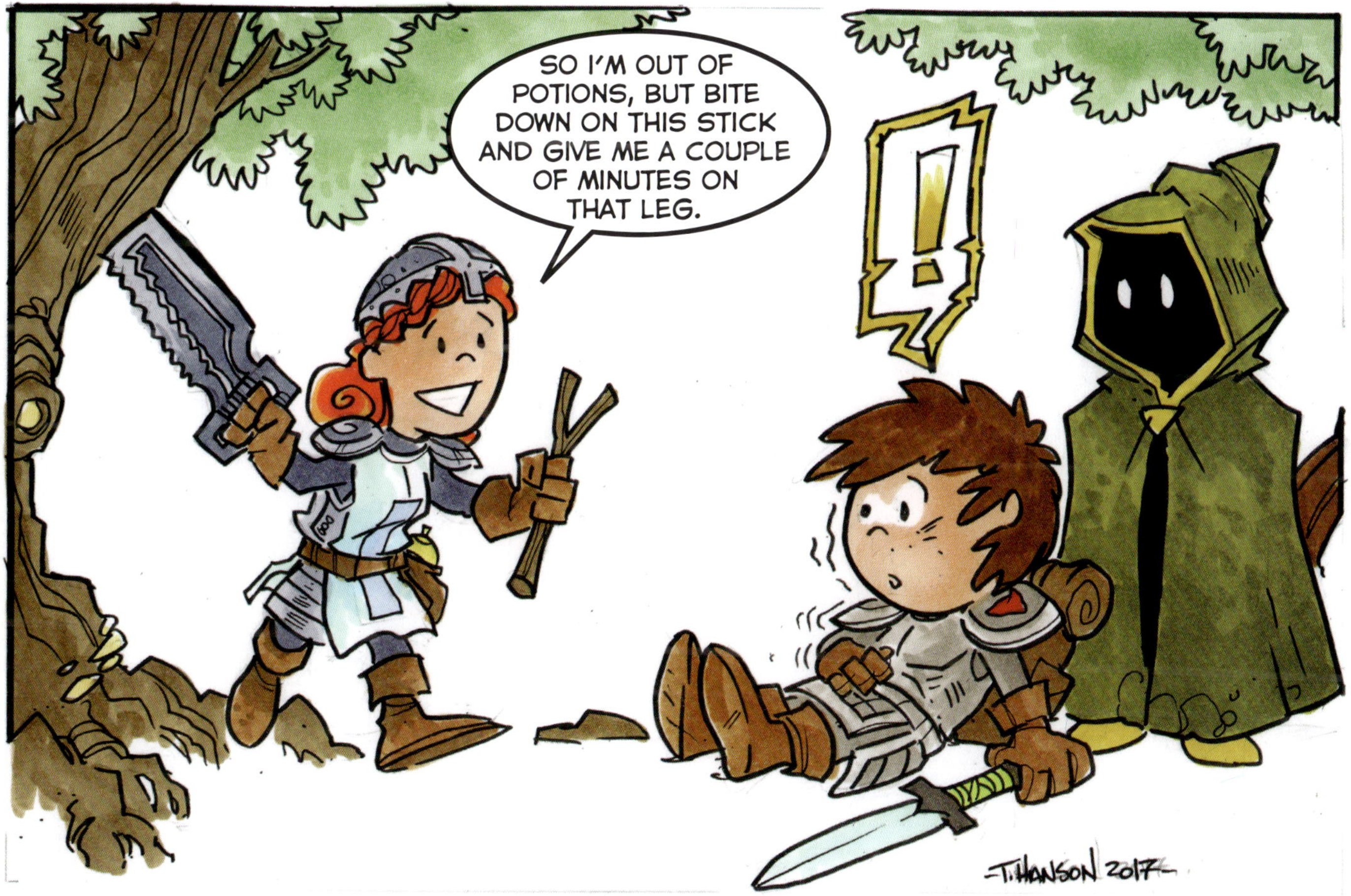

Life of the Party: Realities of an RPG'er

by Travis Hanson

REALLY!?! RIGHT NOW??

HELLO? HELLO?

Life of the Party: Realities of an RPG'er

by Travis Hanson

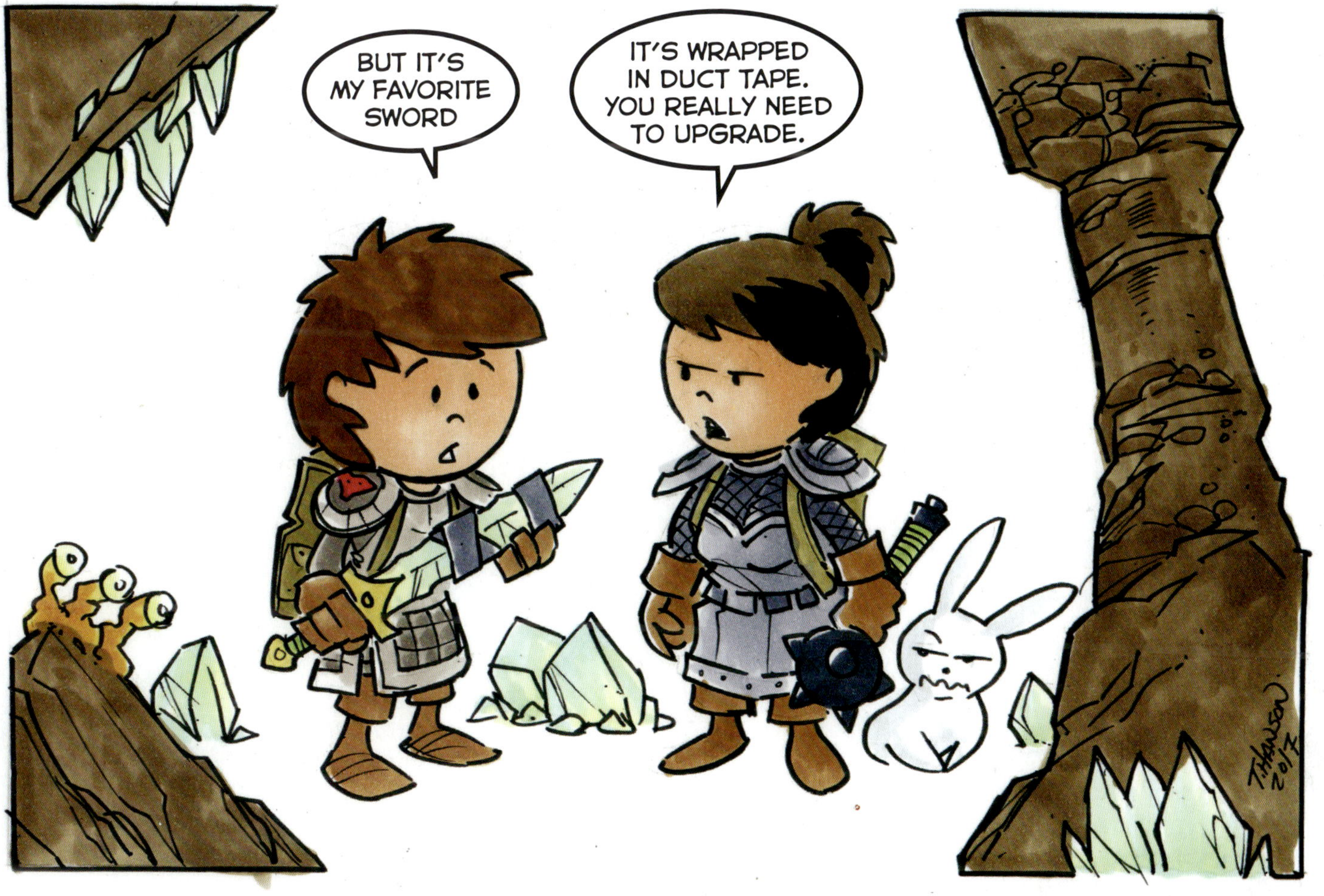

Life of the Party: Realities of an RPG'er

by Travis Hanson

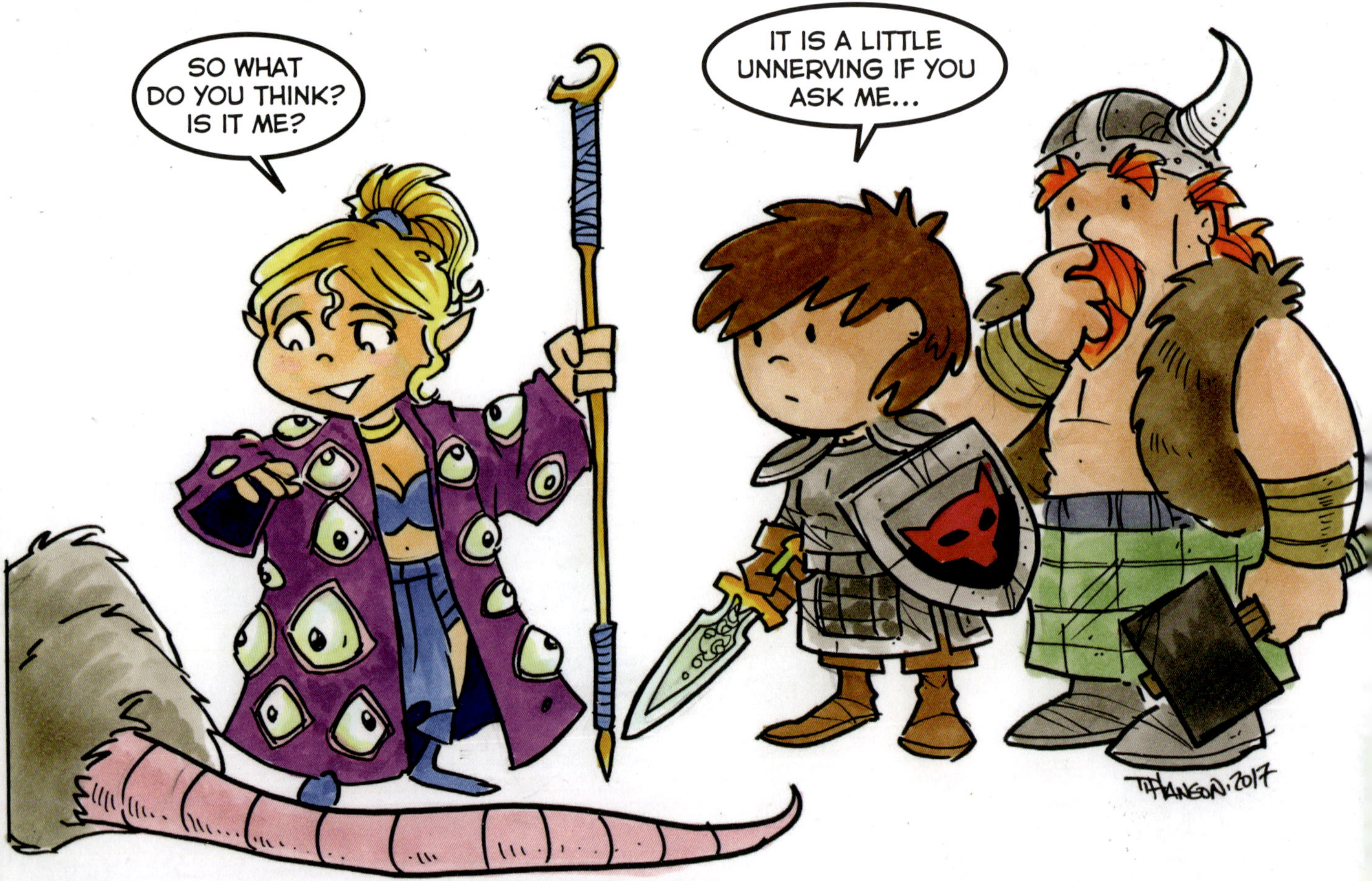

Life of the Party: Realities of an RPG'er by Travis Hanson

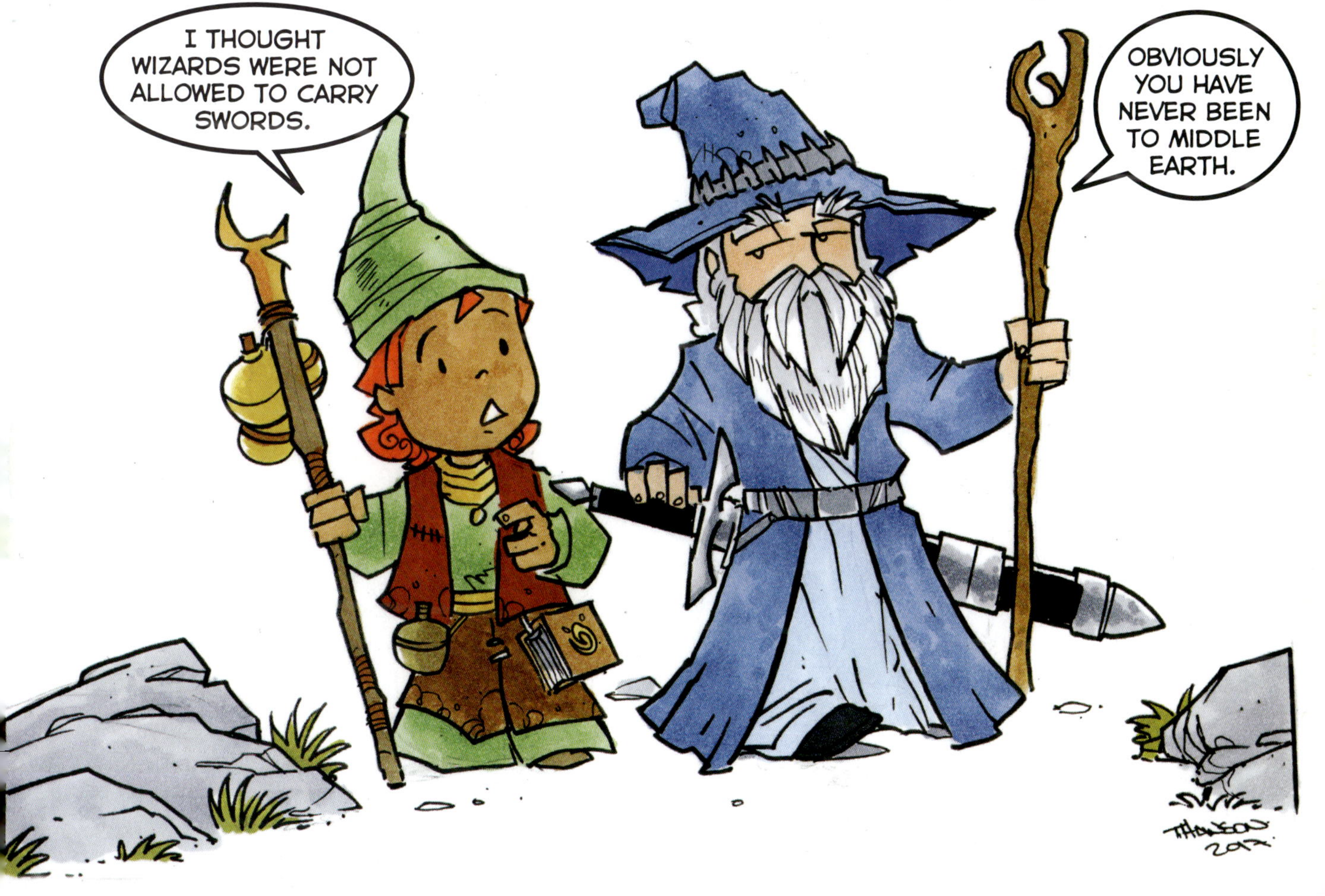

Life of the Party: Realities of an RPG'er

by Travis Hanson

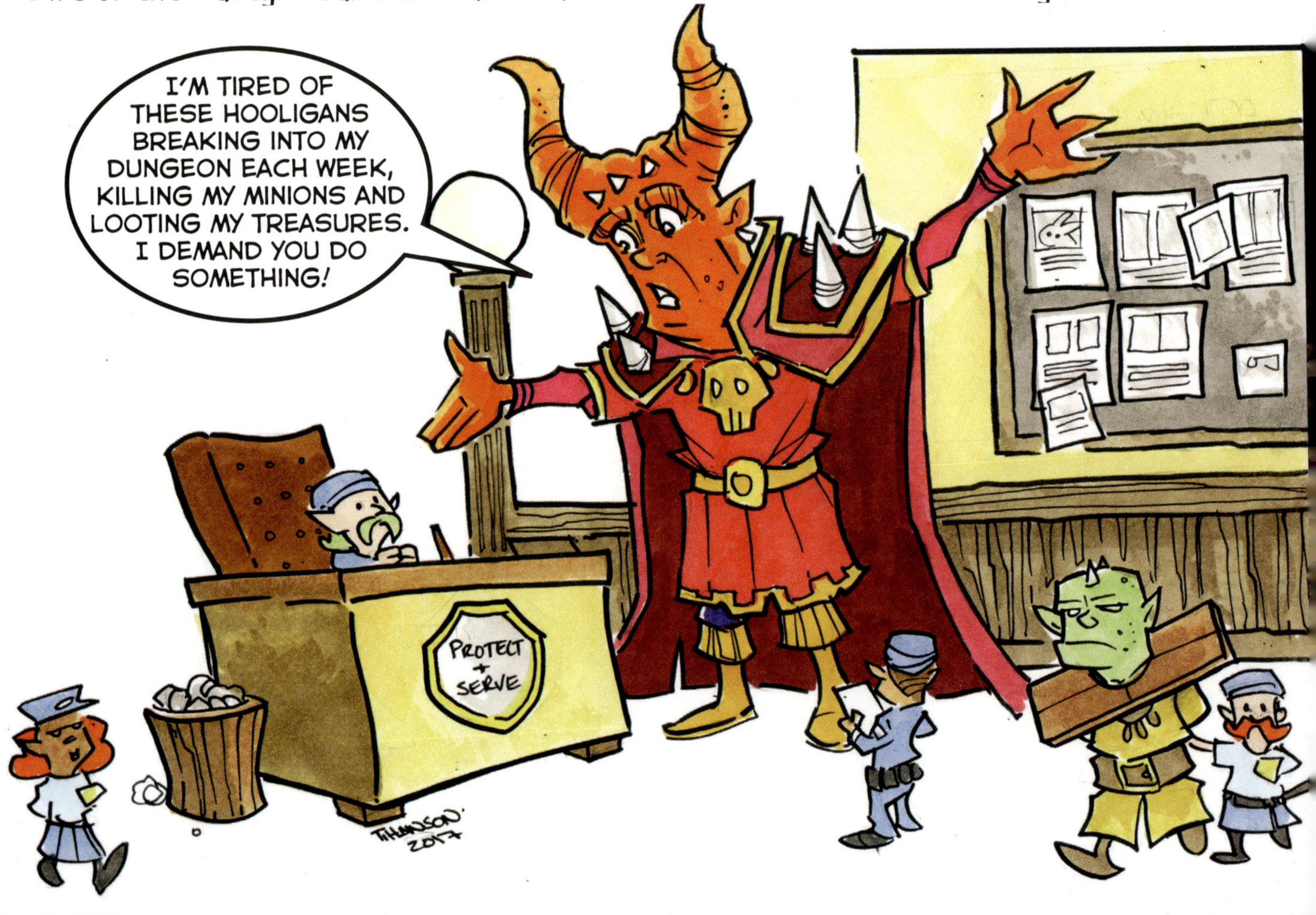

Life of the Party: Realities of an RPG'er

by Travis Hanson

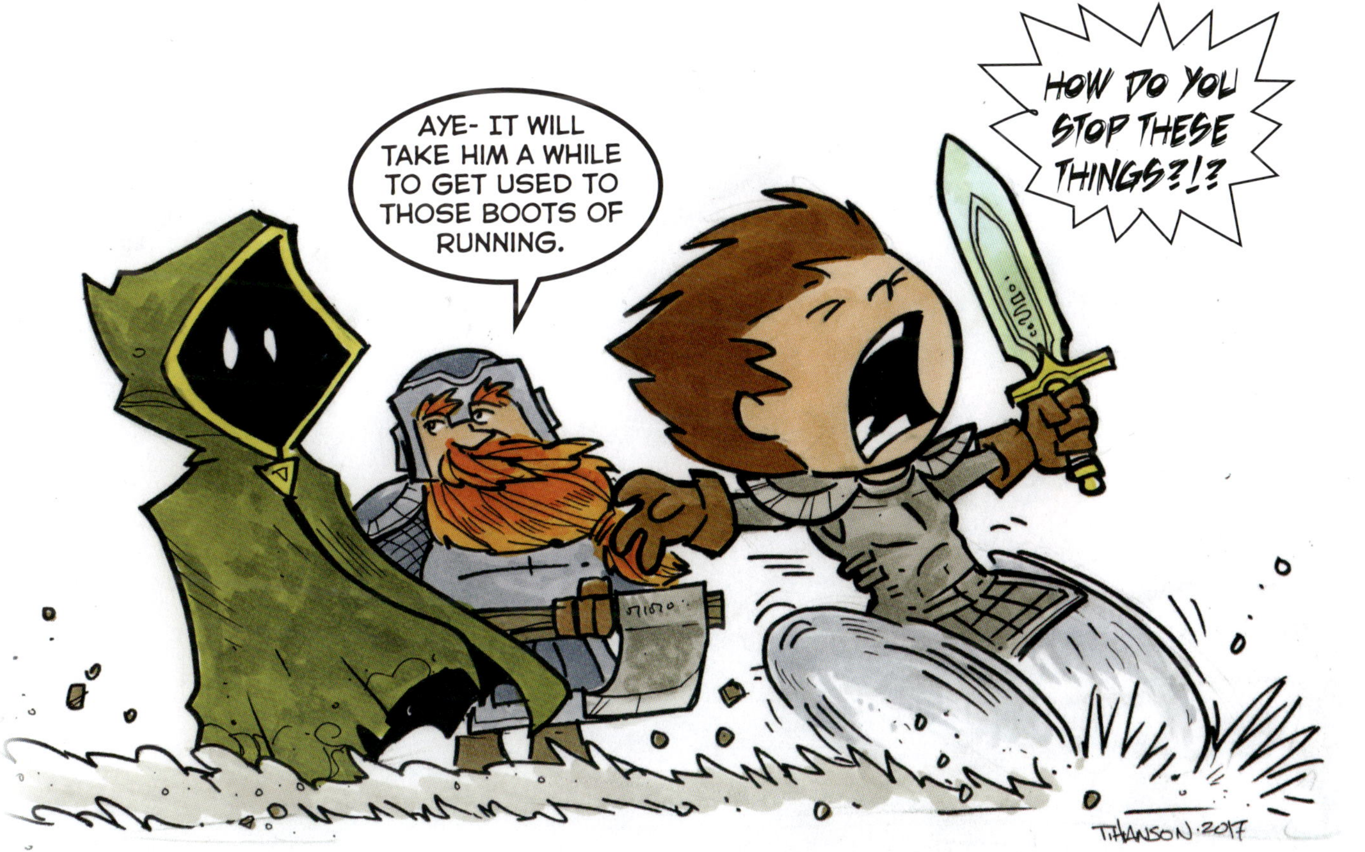

Life of the Party: Realities of an RPG'er

by Travis Hanson

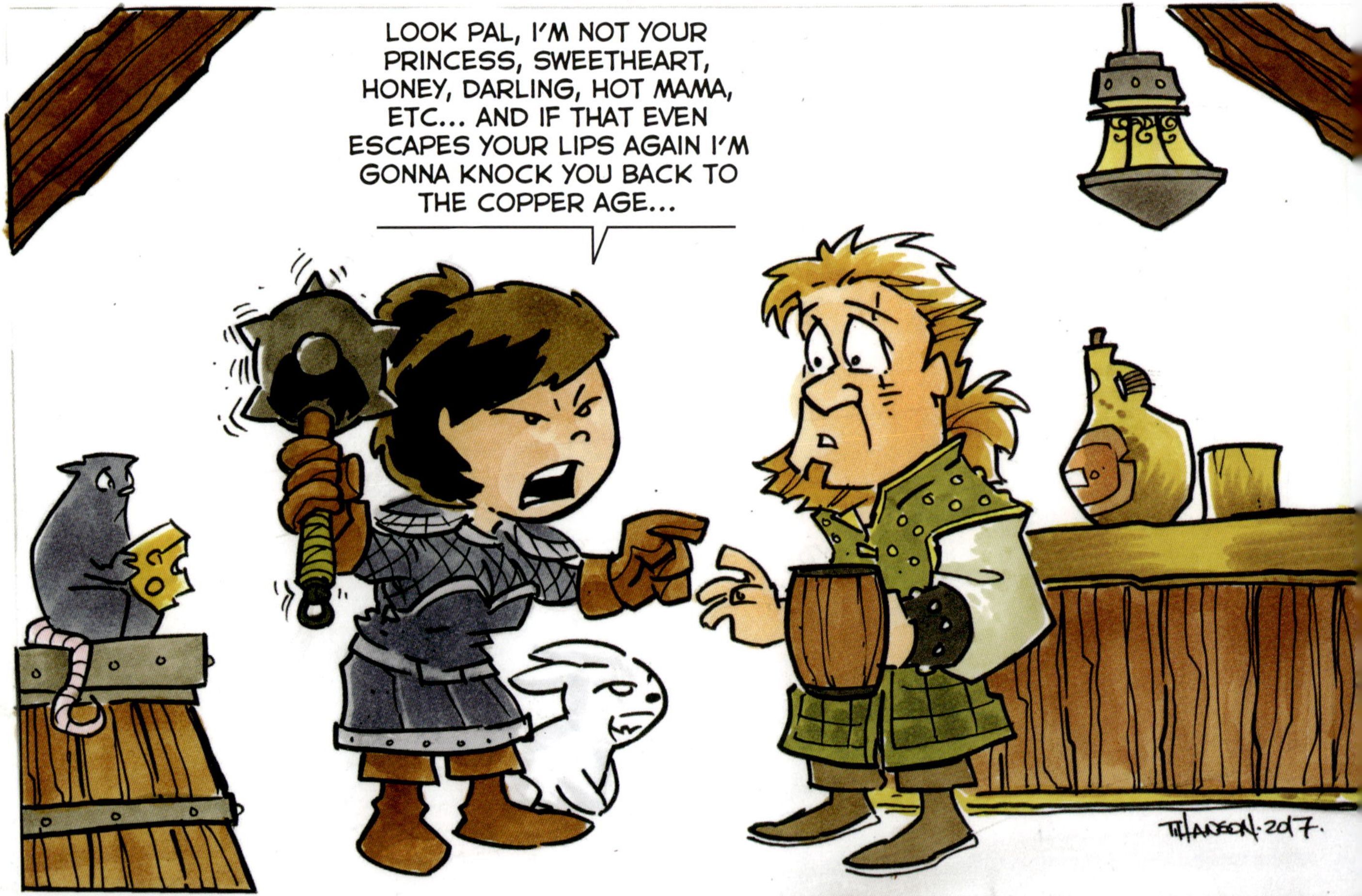

Life of the Party: Realities of an RPG'er

by Travis Hanson

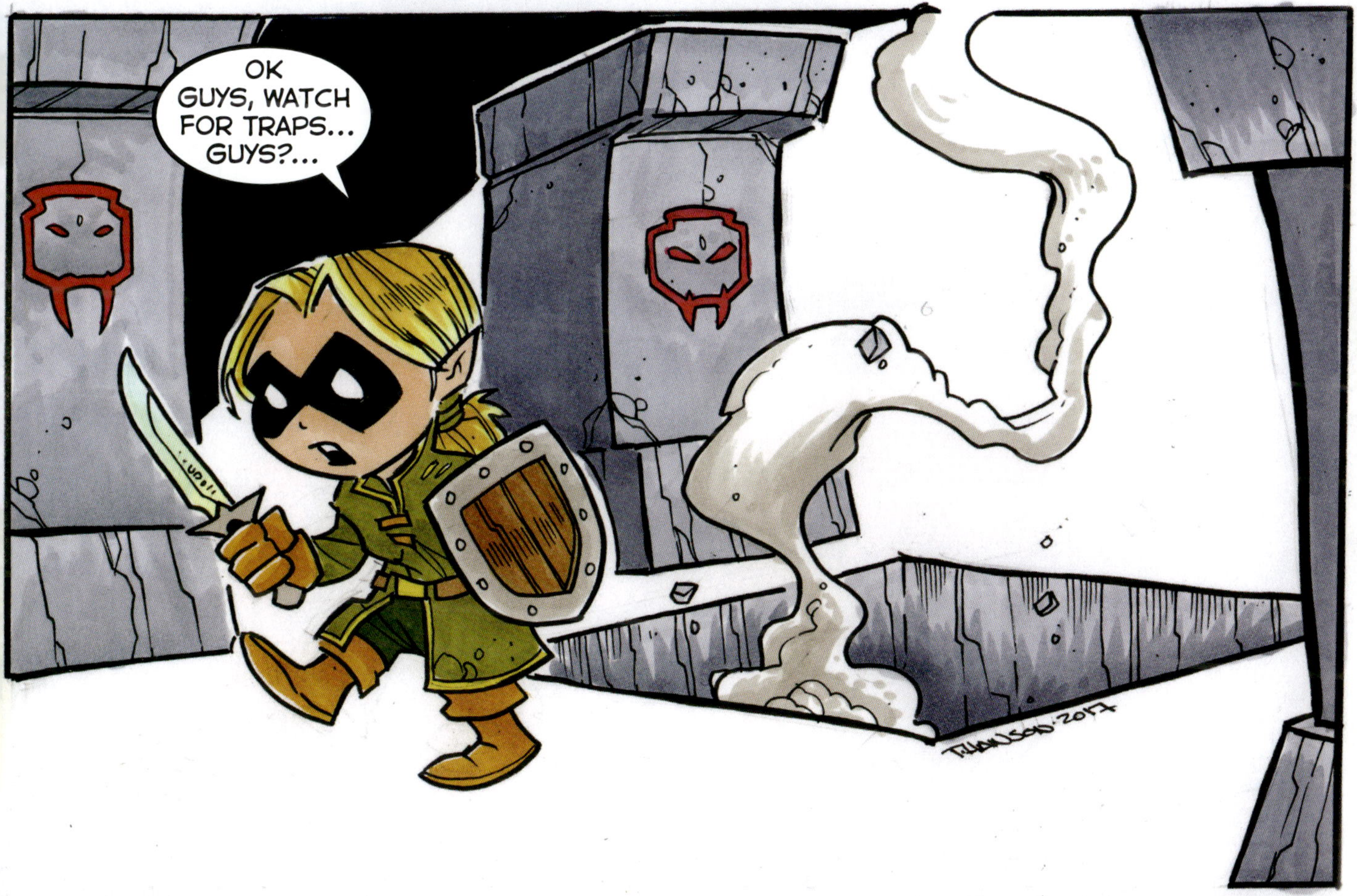

Sketches, Concepts and other Meyhem....

ONE OF MY FAVORITE CARTOONISTS ONCE SAID THAT IF YOU DON'T WRITE DOWN AN IDEA, YOU WILL LOSE IT WITHIN THE HOUR. EVERY CARTOON, IDEA, DESIGN MUST START FROM SOMEWHERE. SOMETIMES IT'S A SIMPLE TAGLINE WRITTEN ON A PIECE OF PAPER, OTHER TIMES IT'S A FLESHED OUT SKETCH. THOUGH HOWEVER IT COMES, IT IS IMPORTANT THAT IT IS WRITTEN DOWN. I BELIEVE THIS TO BE TRUE. LIFE OF THE PARTY IS A MIX OF MY LOVE OF GAMING, FANTASY AND SCI-FI STORIES AND MY LOVE OF CARTOONING. THANK YOU FOR JOINING ME ON THE MOST INCREDIBLE CAMPAIGN, I HAVE EVER EMBARKED ON...

NOW FOR A LITTLE Q&A WITH TRAV-

DO YOU HAVE A FAVORITE RPG?
MY FAVORITE RPG IS ACTUALLY AN OLD ONE CALLED GANGBUSTERS. WE PLAYED IT ALL THE TIME.

WHY DON'T YOU NAME YOUR CHARACTERS?
I FOUND THAT IT WAS IT EASIER FOR PEOPLE TO RELATE TO CHARACTERS WHEN THEY RECOGNIZED THE CLASS INSTEAD OF THE NAME. SO I FELT THAT THE NAME WAS UNIMPORTANT BECAUSE YOU ALREADY HAVE NAMES FOR THEM.

WHAT ARE MY HOBBIES?
I MUST ADMIT... DRAWING, ALTHOUGH I DO LOVE TO COOK AND READ BOOKS. I REALLY LOVE HISTORY BOOKS.

DO YOU GM OR PLAY?
IT'S BEEN A BIT SINCE I HAVE BEEN A GM, BUT I DO LOVE TO DO BOTH.

WHAT GOT YOU INTO RPGS?
AN 8TH GRADE SCIENCE TEACHER AT ORVILLE WRIGHT JR HIGH IN THE EARLY 80'S. HE RAN THE FANTASY AND SCIENCE FICTION CLUB AT LUNCH. I WENT ONE DAY AND I WAS HOOKED.

HOW MUCH OF LIFE HAS IMITATED ART, IMITATING LIFE?
A LOT OF MY STORIES AND ART PIECES HAVE COME FROM MY GAMING EXPERIENCES AS WELL AS OTHERS'. PLUS HAVING HAD THE CHANCE TO WORK ON A FEW RPG GAMES OVER THE YEARS HAS ONLY FUELED MY PASSION FOR MERGING ART AND STORY TELLING.

WHAT WAS THE FIRST GAME/RPG YOU PLAYED?
ADVANCED DUNGEON & DRAGONS, BUT YOU CAN ALSO THROW IN GAMMA WORLDS, GANGBUSTERS AND STAR FRONTIERS. (I KNOW I JUST DATED MYSELF)

WHAT'S YOUR FAVORITE RPG NOW?
MY FAVORITE RPG RIGHT NOW IS ACTUALLY A VIDEO GAME... FINAL FANTASY 9. BUT, I STILL LOVE A GOOD D&D SESSION.

WHAT CLASS DO YOU LIKE TO PLAY? WHAT CLASS DO YOU WANT TO PLAY THAT YOU HAVEN'T YET?
I LIKE ELVEN ROGUES, RANGERS AND THIEVES. AS FOR A CLASS I HAVE NOT PLAYED YET, WHILE I AM INTRIGUED BY THE MONKS, AND I WOULD PLAY A CLERIC, BUT ONLY IF I GET TO HAVE A HOLY HAND GRENADE.

WHAT IS YOUR FAVORITE PART ABOUT THE GAME?
UTILIZING ONE'S IMAGINATION AND THE STORIES THAT CAN COME OUT OF IT. MY BEAN SERIES WAS ACTUALLY PARTS OF CAMPAIGNS I PLAYED YEARS AGO.

IF YOU WROTE YOUR OWN CAMPAIGN WHAT WOULD IT BE ABOUT?
IT WOULD BE A GRITTY SURVIVAL FANTASY GAME: YOU FIGHTING YOUR WAY OUT OF A DUNGEON OR A CASTLE THAT IS UNDER ATTACK. I LIKE MY GAMES TO HAVE A SENSE OF URGENCY AND SURVIVAL. I'M NOT ABOUT HUGE TREASURES OR POWER, BUT MORE ABOUT JUST STAYING ALIVE.

WHAT IS YOUR MOST MEMORABLE ROLE PLAYING MOMENT?
BEING PENCIL-STABBED IN THE LEG BY A FRUSTRATED DM, AFTER AN ALL-NIGHTER OF PLAYING. THIS WAS WHEN PENCILS WERE MADE OF LEAD AND I ENDED UP HAVING TO GET A TETANUS SHOT BECAUSE OF IT.

WHO WAS YOUR FAVORITE GAMING CHARACTER? AND DID HE/SHE END UP AS A COMIC CHARACTER?
AN ELVEN RANGER NAMED REDBOW, AND YUP HE ENDED UP AS A COMIC BOOK CHARACTER, BUT IN A DIFFERENT SERIES.

WHAT LIFE OF THE PARTY CHARACTER DO YOU MOST RELATE TO?
I RELATE TO SEVERAL OF THEM- SOME MORE THAN OTHERS. THE THIEF AND THE KNIGHT PROBABLY ARE THE CLOSEST TO ME.

WHO IS YOUR FAVORITE CHARACTER?
THE WHITE KILLER RABBIT.

HOW MANY ANIMAL CRACKERS WERE EATEN DURING THE MAKING OF THIS BOOK?
NOT AS MANY AS ONE WOULD THINK... OR AS I WOULD HAVE LIKED... THOSE FROSTED ONES ARE LIKE CRACK.

WHAT IS YOUR FAVORITE D&D EDITION?
1ST EDITION, BUT I AM GETTING INTO 5TH EDITION AND I LIKE WHAT I SEE.

WHICH CHARACTER WOULD YOU MOST LIKE TO MEET IN REAL LIFE?
THE GIRL KNIGHT AND HER RABBIT. I WOULD HAVE SAID THE THIEF, BUT I JUST WOULDN'T TRUST HIM.

WHEN DID YOU START DRAWING?
WHEN I WAS LITTLE- AROUND 6. I DIDN'T TAKE IT SERIOUSLY UNTIL I WAS IN MY EARLY 20'S THOUGH.

WILL THE THIEF EVER SUCCESSFULLY SUCCEED IN NABBING SOMETHING OF VALUE?
WE'LL HAVE TO WAIT AND SEE...HE IS PERSISTENT THOUGH.

WHY DON'T YOU PUT MORE BARDS IN YOUR COMICS? THEY'RE REALLY QUITE INTERESTING CHARACTERS
IT HAS TO BE THE RIGHT JOKE FOR EACH CHARACTER. DON'T WORRY YOU WILL SEE SOME MORE BARDS IN THE NEXT BOOK.

WHAT OTHER PROJECTS DO YOU ENJOY WORKING ON?
I AM WORKING ON FINISHING THE 5TH BOOK OF THE BEAN SERIES, AS WELL AS A FEW OTHER CHILDRENS BOOKS THAT WILL BE COMING DOWN THE PIPELINE. I AM ALSO WORKING ON SEVERAL GAMES AT THE MOMENT FOR A FEW OTHER COMPANIES.

TRAVIS HANSON-

IS AN EISNER-NOMINATED ILLUSTRATOR WITH A HUGE IMAGINATION. TRAVIS SPENDS HIS TIME IN SOUTHERN CALIFORNIA, WITH HIS LOVELY WIFE JANELL, 5 CHILDREN AND TWO CATS.